Near Field Communication with Android Cookbook

Discover the endless possibilities of using Android NFC capabilities to enhance your apps over 50 practical recipes

Vitor Subtil

BIRMINGHAM - MUMBAI

Near Field Communication with Android Cookbook

First published: June 2014

Production Reference: 1060614

Published by Packt Publishing Ltd.
Livery Place
35 Livery Street
Birmingham B3 2PB, UK.

ISBN 978-1-78328-965-3

www.packtpub.com

Cover Image by Ravaji Babu (ravaji_babu@outlook.com)

Credits

Author
Vitor Subtil

Reviewers
Dion Loughry
Michael Roland

Commissioning Editor
Kunal Parikh

Acquisition Editor
Rebecca Youé

Content Development Editors
Athira Laji
Rikshith Shetty

Technical Editors
Shubhangi Dhamgaye
Novina Kewalramani
Pratik More
Pratish Soman

Copy Editors
Alisha Aranha
Mradula Hegde
Adithi Shetty

Project Coordinator
Wendell Palmer

Proofreaders
Simran Bhogal
Maria Gould
Ameesha Green
Paul Hindle

Indexer
Mariammal Chettiyar

Production Coordinator
Adonia Jones

Cover Work
Adonia Jones

About the Author

Vitor Subtil has been a web developer since 2009 and has been working with ASP.NET, C#, Oracle, and FluentNhibernate in the development of Enterprise Management applications. He started using MVC and SOA quite recently.

He is currently pursuing his final year graduate studies in Computer Engineering, where he got introduced to the NFC technology and became a fan thereafter.

He is enthusiastic about new technologies such as HTML5, CSS3, and Android. He loves using the JQuery framework for JavaScript programming and uses new features of HTML5 such as OfflineStorage, the History API, and Canvas. His current focus is on developing Android applications.

I would like to thank my girlfriend, Sandra, for all the time she spent helping me and all that she did for me in some difficult situations that occurred while writing this book. This book would have not been possible without her.

About the Reviewers

Dion Loughry has been professionally involved in the IT field for nearly 20 years now. While he has been managing the support for end users for the most of his career, he has always stayed on top of cutting-edge technology and innovation. He has incorporated this habit as much as possible into his personal life and business as well. A great example of this was when he first saw a PC in 1980. He managed to save and borrow enough money to purchase one at that time. In addition, he quickly learned how to program in the BASIC language. His passion lies in using new technology at the workplace to improve efficiency as well as simplify life in general. NFC technology is the next great leap that provides a simplified way of sharing and obtaining information. He has been involved with the NFC technology for a number of years. He has always been a fan of Palm Technology and has worked with a few members of the original Palm development team. He is currently working on many applications for Android and Windows devices. This is a great step into the world of unplugged computing technology and information sharing, which has great potential, yet is widely untapped.

Michael Roland is a researcher at the NFC Research Lab, Hagenberg (University of Applied Sciences, Upper Austria). His main research interests are NFC, security, and Android. He is the creator of NFC TagInfo, one of the most successful NFC developer tools for Android devices, and the co-author of the book *Anwendungen und Technik von Near Field Communication (NFC)*, *Springer Publishing*. He holds a BSc. and an MSc. degree in Embedded Systems Design (University of Applied Sciences, Upper Austria, 2007 and 2009, respectively) and a PhD. (Dr. Techn.) degree in Computer Science (Johannes Kepler University Linz, 2013).

www.PacktPub.com

Support files, eBooks, discount offers, and more

You might want to visit www.PacktPub.com for support files and downloads related to your book.

Did you know that Packt offers eBook versions of every book published, with PDF and ePub files available? You can upgrade to the eBook version at www.PacktPub.com and as a print book customer, you are entitled to a discount on the eBook copy. Get in touch with us at service@packtpub.com for more details.

At www.PacktPub.com, you can also read a collection of free technical articles, sign up for a range of free newsletters and receive exclusive discounts and offers on Packt books and eBooks.

http://PacktLib.PacktPub.com

Do you need instant solutions to your IT questions? PacktLib is Packt's online digital book library. Here, you can access, read and search across Packt's entire library of books.

Why Subscribe?

- Fully searchable across every book published by Packt
- Copy and paste, print and bookmark content
- On demand and accessible via web browser

Free Access for Packt account holders

If you have an account with Packt at www.PacktPub.com, you can use this to access PacktLib today and view nine entirely free books. Simply use your login credentials for immediate access.

Table of Contents

Preface

Mobile technologies are constantly changing, providing users with faster and better ways to interact with the world. Devices and applications have become increasingly powerful and new technologies are continually emerging—near field communication (NFC) is one of them. Its low battery consumption and simplicity are the key factors determining its future success. From facilitating daily tasks, such as opening a website, gaining access control, and making instant payments, NFC is now being used everywhere. Features such as peer-to-peer communication, cross-device data exchange, social network content sharing, and improved gaming experiences can be achieved using NFC.

The book begins by introducing the virtual development environment that allows you to develop NFC-enabled applications without the need of a smartphone or tags. Next, this book presents simple and functional examples that explain the basic concepts of detecting, writing, and reading data from a tag. All of the presented features and techniques are then used in a more complex application to give you a better idea of how you can use NFC in a real application.

In this book, you will learn how to use different components and features, such as working with the Foreground Dispatch System, using the NFC data exchange format and the Android application record, reading and writing a URI, creating text and customizing mime NDEF messages, and so on. This book provides readers with both theoretical and practical knowledge as we progress through the recipes and explain the relevant concepts.

Toward the end of this book, the recipes will show you various ways to use NFC so that you will be pumped to start developing amazing NFC applications.

What this book covers

Chapter 1, Getting Started with NFC, covers the basic steps to create an NFC-enabled application by defining the minimum requirements and the first lines of code needed to use NFC. This chapter also covers how to set up a virtual test environment using Open NFC for an Android add-on.

Chapter 2, Detecting a Tag, introduces readers to the detection, interception, and filtering of NFC intents, using the Foreground Dispatch System and intent filters. A technical overview of the different types of tags and a series of practical examples explains how you could go about doing this.

Chapter 3, Writing Tag Content, covers the introduction to the NDEF records by explaining how this format is useful and the different possible usages. This chapter provides practical working examples that demonstrate the correct NDEF usage.

Chapter 4, Writing Tag Content – Real-life Examples, provides more detailed examples on writing different content to NFC tags by providing working application prototypes.

Chapter 5, Reading Tag Content, introduces the reading of an NFC tag content and how to handle different types of content.

Chapter 6, Reading Tag Content – Real-life Examples, covers more detailed examples on reading tag content. At the end of every recipe, a working application is created to provide insight into the NFC capabilities.

Chapter 7, Sharing Content across Devices, covers a more advanced NFC feature, peer-to-peer communication. This chapter provides working application prototypes that demonstrate how the NFC peer-to-peer feature can be used in gaming and social networking applications.

Chapter 8, Error Handling and Content Validation, covers the basics on how to prevent the NFC application from crashing by correctly handling and preventing exceptions.

Chapter 9, Extending NFC, covers how NFC can be used to complement other Android features by providing practical working examples of applications that facilitate a user's interaction with the world.

Chapter 10, Real-life Examples – NFC Utilities, covers some tips on how to make the best use of an NFC tag. This chapter also provides a working application prototype to allow for a full-learning experience.

What you need for this book

Readers must have basic knowledge of Java and Android application development.

An NFC-enabled device and physical tags are recommended but not required. This is because readers can use the virtual environment to administer development tests.

The software used during the writing of this book was Eclipse, so we recommend a working installation that is configured with Android SDK.

Who this book is for

Near Field Communication with Android Cookbook focuses on employing NFC features in useful, real-life applications. It is ideal for developers who want to learn how to create NFC-enabled Android applications. Basic Android development knowledge is preferred, but the main objective is to get readers excited about this technology! We do this by providing you with a solid grounding in the use of NFC with Android as well as some advanced examples.

Conventions

In this book, you will find a number of styles of text that distinguish between different kinds of information. Here are some examples of these styles, and an explanation of their meaning.

Code words in text, database table names, folder names, filenames, file extensions, pathnames, dummy URLs, user input, and Twitter handles are shown as follows: "`nfcbook.ch1.example1.`"

A block of code is set as follows:

```
NfcAdapter nfcAdapter = NfcAdapter.getDefaultAdapter(this);

if (nfcAdapter != null && nfcAdapter.isEnabled()) {
  Toast.makeText(this, "NFC is available.", Toast.LENGTH_LONG).
show();
} else {
  Toast.makeText(this, "NFC is not available on this device. This
application may not work correctly.",
Toast.LENGTH_LONG).show();
}
```

When we wish to draw your attention to a particular part of a code block, the relevant lines or items are set in bold:

```
<uses-permission android:name="android.permission.NFC" />
```

New terms and **important words** are shown in bold. Words that you see on the screen, in menus or dialog boxes for example, appear in the text like this: "A **Beam sent!** toast should appear in the touched device and a Facebook friend request dialog should appear in the other."

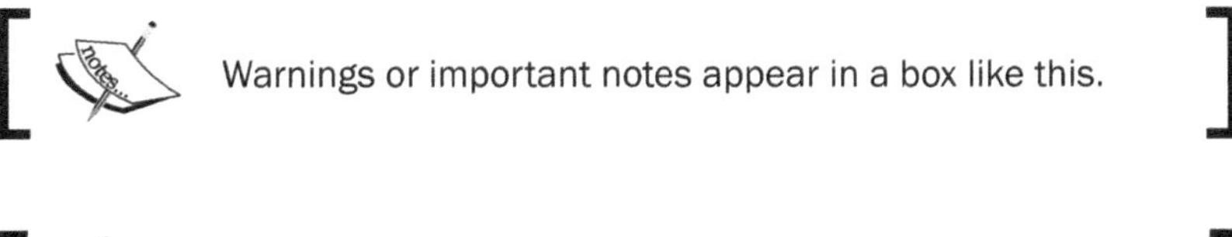

Warnings or important notes appear in a box like this.

Tips and tricks appear like this.

Reader feedback

Feedback from our readers is always welcome. Let us know what you think about this book—what you liked or may have disliked. Reader feedback is important for us to develop titles that you really get the most out of.

To send us general feedback, simply send an e-mail to `feedback@packtpub.com`, and mention the book title via the subject of your message.

If there is a topic that you have expertise in and you are interested in either writing or contributing to a book, see our author guide on `www.packtpub.com/authors`.

Customer support

Now that you are the proud owner of a Packt book, we have a number of things to help you to get the most from your purchase.

Downloading the example code

You can download the example code files for all Packt books you have purchased from your account at `http://www.packtpub.com`. If you purchased this book elsewhere, you can visit `http://www.packtpub.com/support` and register to have the files e-mailed directly to you.

Errata

Although we have taken every care to ensure the accuracy of our content, mistakes do happen. If you find a mistake in one of our books—maybe a mistake in the text or the code—we would be grateful if you would report this to us. By doing so, you can save other readers from frustration and help us improve subsequent versions of this book. If you find any errata, please report them by visiting `http://www.packtpub.com/submit-errata`, selecting your book, clicking on the **errata submission form** link, and entering the details of your errata. Once your errata are verified, your submission will be accepted and the errata will be uploaded on our website, or added to any list of existing errata, under the Errata section of that title. Any existing errata can be viewed by selecting your title from `http://www.packtpub.com/support`.

Piracy

Piracy of copyright material on the Internet is an ongoing problem across all media. At Packt, we take the protection of our copyright and licenses very seriously. If you come across any illegal copies of our works, in any form, on the Internet, please provide us with the location address or website name immediately so that we can pursue a remedy.

Please contact us at `copyright@packtpub.com` with a link to the suspected pirated material.

We appreciate your help in protecting our authors, and our ability to bring you valuable content.

Questions

You can contact us at `questions@packtpub.com` if you are having a problem with any aspect of the book, and we will do our best to address it.

1

Getting Started with NFC

In this chapter, we will cover the following topics:

- Requesting NFC permissions
- Indicating that your app uses NFC
- Defining minimal requirements
- Verifying whether the device has an NFC controller
- Downloading Open NFC Android Edition
- Downloading Open NFC SDK Edition
- Configuring the Open NFC Android add-on into your Android SDK
- Configuring an NFC-enabled testing AVD
- Configuring the Connection Center tool
- Testing your app all together

Introduction

We live in a world that is constantly changing, and every day, new and innovative technologies emerge which make daily life easier and more convenient. **Near Field Communication** (**NFC**) is one of these new technologies. It allows users to exchange digital content between devices with a simple touch. It is a short-range RFID technology that is currently being introduced in smartphones and used for mobile payments, mobile ticketing, marketing, identification mechanisms, and other such cool applications.

NFC is specified by the NFC Forum, `http://nfc-forum.org/`, which promotes the implementation and definition of the NFC standards for interoperability of devices and services. The biggest differences among the common RFID technologies are the communication distance, which is limited to about 10 centimeters, and the ability for bidirectional communication.

By now, you are probably thinking, why do I need another adapter on my smartphone? This will be another battery-draining feature that most probably will be disabled most of the time. Well, that's not exactly the case when we talk about NFC. It is specially designed to have a very small battery consumption footprint so that it can be enabled all the time, thus avoiding the annoying rituals of enabling and disabling the adapter when we need to use it.

However, you might think you can't send large amounts of data; that's true, but it doesn't matter! We already have other good and reliable alternatives such as Bluetooth or Wi-Fi Direct for that. So, why would we need another super-fast, battery-drainer adapter? With NFC, things are kept simple. There's no need to pair devices, it can be constantly turned on, and it takes less than one-tenth of a second to establish a connection between devices.

Then you may think that what you really want is to keep the battery consumption low and still be able to transfer bigger files. In cases like these, we can use the best of both worlds. For example, we can use NFC to transfer a small data block that contains the necessary information for a successful Bluetooth pair, then turn Bluetooth on, pair the devices, transfer the files, and turn it off again. All of this is done automatically and with a seamless user experience. That too with just one tap!

NFC communication can be established between two NFC-enabled devices or between a device and a tag. One of the entities in the communication process will act as **active** and will be responsible for sending, reading, or writing the data, and the other will act as **passive**. There are three main operation modes:

- **Reading and writing**: In this mode, a device reads and writes data to/from a tag.

- **Peer to Peer (P2P)**: In this mode, a P2P connection is established between two devices.

- **Host Card Emulation (HCE)**: In this mode, a device emulates the behavior of a tag/card. For example, we can use our smartphone as if we are using several payment cards.

This book will focus only on the first two modes. HCE is available from Android 4.4 KitKat, onwards and you should have a look at this amazing feature at `http://developer.android.com/guide/topics/connectivity/nfc/hce.html`

In this first chapter, we will create a very simple application that will allow us to cover the first steps needed in all applications that use NFC, as well as cover how to set up a working virtual testing environment.

Requesting NFC permissions

As Android developers, we are accustomed to using the manifest file to request permission to use a specific device feature, and NFC is no exception to this.

Getting ready

Make sure you have an NFC-enabled Android device or a virtual test environment—refer to the *Testing your app all together* recipe.

How to do it...

We will start by creating an Android project where we will request the correct permissions, as shown in the following steps:

1. Open Eclipse and create a new Android application project named `NfcBookCh1Example1` and a package named `nfcbook.ch1.example1`, as shown in the following screenshot:

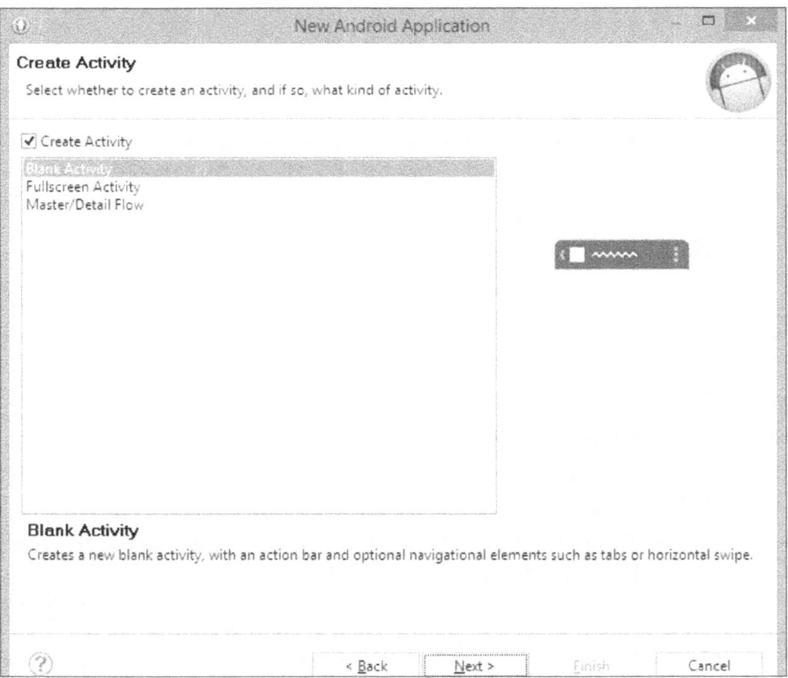

2. Make sure you select **API 10: Android 2.3.3 (GingerBread)** in the **Minimum Required SDK** field.

3. When prompted to create an activity, select **Blank Activity**.

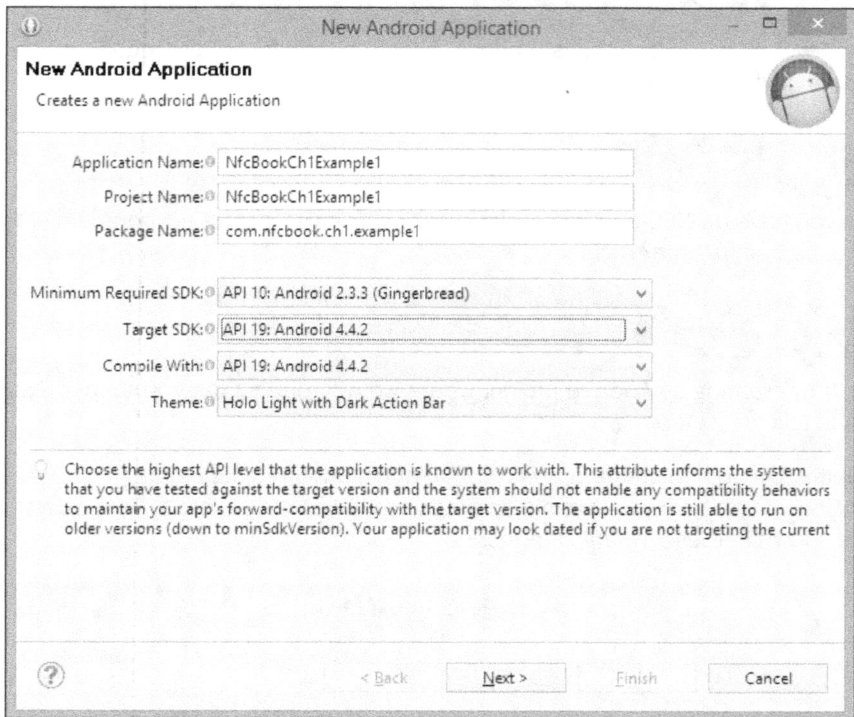

4. Open the `AndroidManifest.xml` file located in the project's root and add the following code just before the application node:

```
<uses-permission android:name="android.permission.NFC"/>
```

How it works...

Android requires every app to request permissions from the user to allow the application to perform restricted actions. Examples of restricted actions include access to users' current location, permission to send an SMS without user interaction permission to, read contacts, and many others. This is done in the `AndroidManifest.xml` file using the `<uses-permission/>` node. Permissions are granted by the user when the application is installed. Requesting unnecessary permissions may cause users to not trust the application and refrain from installation. If we do not request permissions in the manifest and try to do restricted actions, an exception is thrown and the application will not work correctly.

Indicating that your app uses NFC

This step isn't required, but it is always good practice to specify the features used in our app manifest file—if it is indeed a required feature for our application to work correctly. Google Play Store uses this information to filter the apps visible to users based on their device's specifications. Users with incompatible devices will be able to install the application if we don't specify this, and we don't want that. We don't want users to get frustrated with a non-working application and give us negative feedback.

How to do it...

We are going to continue adding functionality to the previously created project by declaring the features required by our application in the manifest as follows:

1. Open the `NfcBookCh1Example1` project created in the previous recipe.
2. Open the `AndroidManifest.xml` file located in the project root and add the following code just before the application node. Since NFC is a required feature in our application, we should also set the required attribute to `true`, as shown in the following line of code:

```
<uses-feature android:name="android.hardware.nfc"
   android:required="true" />
```

How it works...

The Android market uses this information in the manifest to filter the apps visible to the users. This way, if your device doesn't support a required feature of an app, there's no need for that app to appear listed; it will still be listed on the website but we cannot install it since it's incompatible. This application node is not required, but it's a good idea to place it. Otherwise, the user will be disappointed with the app—it will probably just crash or show an `an error occurred!` message. Users don't like that, and this results in a bad rating.

An alternative is to have multiple approaches for the same result. For example, if the user's device isn't NFC enabled, use a QR code instead (when applicable).

Defining minimal requirements

Defining minimal requirements is a very important step since only users with minimal requirements will be able to run our application properly.

NFC was introduced in Android Version 2.3, API level 9, although some very important features, such as being able to get an instance of the NFC Adapter, were only introduced in API level 10. This is the minimum API level we can work with. Users with previous versions of Android will not be able to use our NFC applications unless a fallback alternative is added.

How to do it...

We are going to define the minimum required version of Android to enable our application to use NFC features, as follows:

1. Open the previously created `NfcBookCh1Example1` project.
2. Set the minimum SDK version to `10` with the following code:

```
<uses-sdk android:minSdkVersion="10" />
```

How it works...

When we add the previous line to the manifest file, Eclipse will automatically scan our code and warn us of incompatible pieces of code. This is also used in the market to filter searches for apps that our devices are able to run. NFC-related features are consistently being added and improved in the latest Android releases; so, depending on your application specifications, you may need to target a higher version.

Verifying whether the device has an NFC adapter

The very first lines of code we write in an app that uses NFC should be a simple validation that tests for the NFC adapter.

How to do it...

We'll create an application that shows a *Toast* saying whether the device has the NFC adapter, as follows:

1. Open the previously created `NfcBookCh1Example1` project.
2. Open `MainActivity` located under `nfcbook.ch1.example1` and place the following code inside the `onCreate` method:

```
NfcAdapter nfcAdapter = NfcAdapter.getDefaultAdapter(this);

if (nfcAdapter != null && nfcAdapter.isEnabled()) {
  Toast.makeText(this, "NFC is available.", Toast.LENGTH_LONG).
show();
} else {
  Toast.makeText(this, "NFC is not available on this device.
This application may not work correctly.",
Toast.LENGTH_LONG).show();
}
```

3. Run the application and try enabling and disabling NFC and see the different results.

How it works...

Android provides a simple way to request the Adapter object by calling `getDefaultAdapter([context])`. If a valid `NfcAdapter` instance is returned, the NFC adapter is available; however, we still need to check if it is enabled by calling the `isEnabled()` method. Otherwise, we need to inform the user that the application may not function correctly as NFC is a required feature. Testing the result for a null value is the simplest way to know if NFC is available to us. However, we can also use the `hasSystemFeature` method from the `PackageManager` class to do this validation.

There's more...

Testing for NFC is an operation that we will probably do very often. So, we can create a simple method and call it every time we need to test for NFC, as shown in the following code:

```java
@Override
protected void onCreate(Bundle savedInstanceState) {
    super.onCreate(savedInstanceState);
    setContentView(R.layout.activity_main);

    if (hasNfc()) {
        Toast.makeText(this, "NFC is available.", Toast.LENGTH_LONG).
show();
    } else {
        Toast.makeText(this, "NFC is not available on this device. This
application may not work correctly.", Toast.LENGTH_LONG).show();
    }
}

boolean hasNfc() {
    boolean hasFeature = getPackageManager().
hasSystemFeature(PackageManager.FEATURE_NFC);
    boolean isEnabled = NfcAdapter.getDefaultAdapter(this).isEnabled();

    return hasFeature && isEnabled;
}
```

Downloading Open NFC Android Edition

Application development using a virtual device is very popular in Android. Using virtual devices lets you use adapters that you may not have in your real device and test your application in several Android versions. The NFC adapter is no exception; so, even if your smartphone isn't an NFC-enabled device, there is no excuse not to use this awesome technology.

Android SDK tools provide us with **Android Virtual Devices** (**AVD**), which are device emulator configurations that allow us to configure hardware and software options. Open NFC Android Edition allows us to create an NFC-enabled AVD since there is no native support for that. We can then simulate a tag tap or a P2P tap, and the correct intent is launched like it would be in a real device.

Getting ready

The following are the settings required for this recipe:

- Make sure you have a working Android development environment. If you don't, ADT Bundle is a good start. You can download it from `http://developer.android.com/sdk/index.html`.
- It is assumed that Eclipse is the development IDE for Android.

How to do it...

We are going to download, extract, and verify the Open NFC files that are needed to get our virtual test environment up and running, as shown in the following steps:

1. Open a new browser window and navigate to `http://open-nfc.org`.
2. On the left navigation menu, click on **Downloads**.
3. On the download list, select the **4.4.1** Open NFC for Android release. The download link's name should be **Android Edition (SDK)**.

   At the time of writing this book, the current Open NFC release is 4.5.2 for Android 4.2.1, Jelly Bean; however, since this version has been reported to be faulty several times, we will use an older but stable version.

4. Create a folder named `NFCBook` in your home directory and extract the downloaded archive.
5. There should be a folder named `android_sdk` and at least one folder named `OpenNFC_AddOn` in it, where we will find an Android image on which we will create our AVD.

Downloading Open NFC SDK Edition

Open NFC SDK Edition allows us to connect to the AVD, log in NFC communications, and simulate different tag taps and P2P taps.

How to do it...

We are going to download, extract, and verify the files used to connect the AVD to the NFC Simulator that allows us to test the NFC application without a physical NFC-enabled device with the following steps:

1. Open a new browser window and navigate to `http://open-nfc.org`.
2. On the left navigation menu, click on **Downloads**.
3. On the download list, select the 4.4.1 SDK release.
4. Extract the downloaded archive to the previously created `NFCBook` directory.
5. There should be a folder named `core` in it and at least two folders named `connection_center` and `nfcc_simulator`. The `nfcc_simulator` folder will allow us to simulate a tag tap or a P2P connection. The `connection_center` folder contains the software that allows the simulator to communicate with the AVD.

Configuring the Open NFC Android add-on into your Android SDK

In this recipe, we will see how to set up the Open NFC Android Edition add-on in our existing Android SDK installation.

Getting ready

The following are the settings required for this recipe:

- Make sure that the Android SDK and the Open NFC add-on target Android version is installed. Since the Open NFC version used is targeting Android ICS 4.0.3, we need to have Android API level 15 installed. Navigate to `https://developer.android.com/sdk/installing/adding-packages.html` for instructions on how to install packages.

- Make sure you have downloaded Open NFC Android Edition—refer to the *Downloading Open NFC Android Edition* recipe.

- It's assumed that the Android SDK location is known and that Open NFC Android Edition was previously downloaded and extracted to the `NFCBook` folder in your home directory.

Downloading the example code

You can download the example code files for all Packt books you have purchased from your account at http://www.packtpub.com. If you purchased this book elsewhere, you can visit http://www.packtpub.com/support and register to have the files e-mailed directly to you.

How to do it...

We are going to configure the previously downloaded Open NFC plugin into our Android SKD installation as follows:

1. Open the `NFCBook` folder and navigate to the `Open NFC for Android Edition` folder.

2. Copy the `add-ons` folder located inside the `OpenNFC_AddOn` folder to your clipboard.

3. Navigate to the Android SDK installation folder.

4. Paste the `add-ons` folder from your clipboard (copied in step 2) to the Android SDK folder. If asked to merge the two folders, select **yes**.

5. Start Android SDK Manager by installing the `SDK Manager.exe` file on Windows. You should see the Open NFC add-on under the Android version item, as shown in the following screenshot:

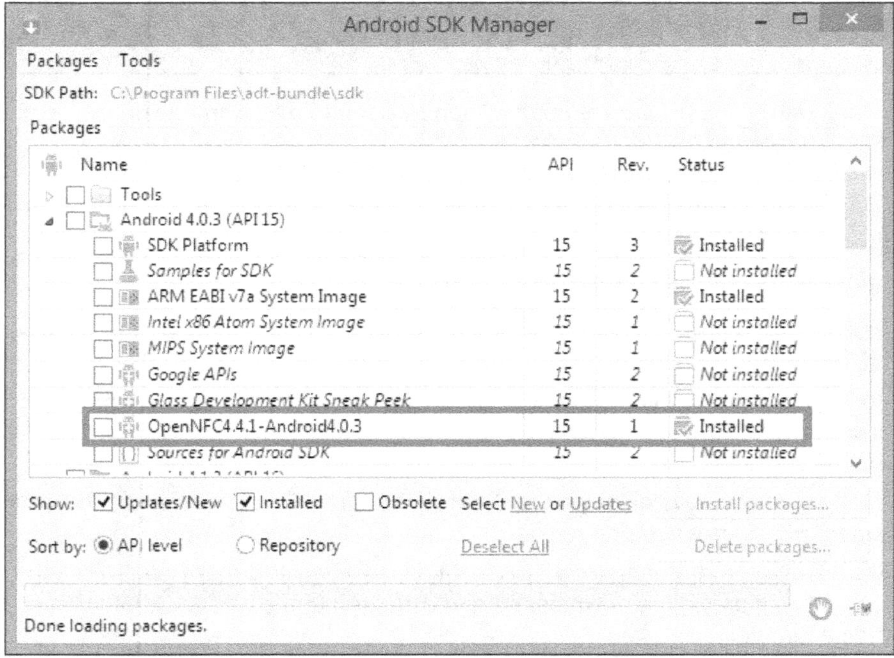

How it works...

The `add-ons` folder in Open NFC Android Edition contains a modified image of the Android system. This modified image contains the simulator for the NFC controller.

Configuring an NFC-enabled testing AVD

We will create and configure an AVD based on the Open NFC Android Edition image. This virtual device will be able to exchange data between the NFC Simulator tool and therefore allows us to test our applications.

Getting ready

The following are the settings required for this recipe:

- Make sure Open NFC Android Edition is properly configured in the Android SDK—refer to the *Configuring the Open NFC Android add-on into your Android SDK* recipe
- Make sure you have downloaded Open NFC SDK Edition—refer to the *Downloading Open NFC SDK Edition* recipe
- It's assumed that the Open NFC SDK Edition Core has been downloaded and extracted to the `NFCBook` folder in your home directory

How to do it...

We are going to use the Android Virtual Device Manager tool to create a device capable of simulating the NFC feature as follows:

1. Open the `NFCBook` folder and navigate to the Android SDK folder.

2. Start **SDK Manager** and navigate to **Tools | Manage AVDs...**.

3. On the **Android Virtual Device Manager** window, click on **New** to open the creation wizard.

4. Configure the parameters as shown in the following screenshot. The **Target** parameter must be Open NFC Android Edition, and the **RAM** should be set to a maximum value of 768 to prevent the AVD from failing to start. Also, **Device** should be set to a standard device and not to Galaxy Nexus or other such specific devices.

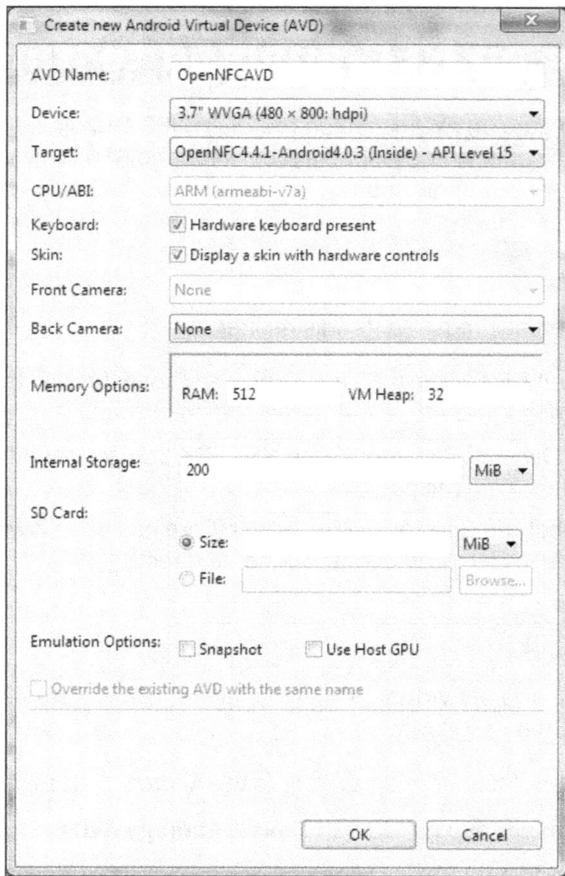

5. Click on **OK** and start the AVD you created.

6. Once the AVD finishes booting, open the application drawer and open the **Settings Open NFC** application, as shown in the following screenshot:

7. Configure the parameters as shown in the following screenshot:

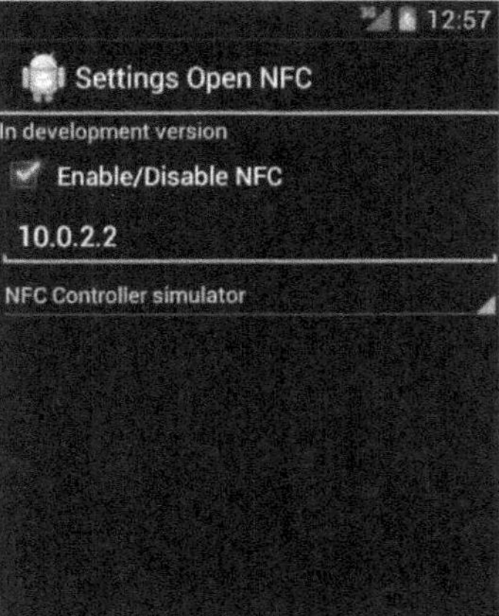

8. Shut down the AVD.

How it works...

When we created the AVD, its target was the modified Android system image; so, when the AVD starts, it also starts the NFC Controller Simulator.

By default, the AVD is configured for the MicroRead controller and NFC is not enabled. We needed to change the configuration to simulator. So, we set the 10.0.2.2 IP address, which is a special alias that represents our machine, and then finally enable NFC.

There's more...

If you have a slower/older PC, or don't like to wait an infinite amount of time for the AVD to start, or you simply do not like the native simulator, there is a pretty neat alternative. Open NFC provides a **VirtualBox** appliance, which allows us to run Android in a virtual machine. It's a much faster and smoother alternative, and no extra configuration is needed.

We need to download an open source virtualization software and create a working Android virtual machine as follows:

1. Download and install VirtualBox from `https://www.virtualbox.org/`.

2. Download the VirtualBox appliance from the **Download** section on the Open NFC website.

3. In VirtualBox, go to **File-Import Appliance** and import the downloaded one from Open NFC.

4. Start the virtual machine and go to **View-Switch to Scale Mode** to fit the window to your screen.

Configuring the Connection Center tool

The Connection Center tool is like a bridge for communication between our AVD and our NFC Simulator. It just needs some simple configuration to provide smooth communication.

Getting ready

The following are the settings required for this recipe:

- Make sure you have downloaded Open NFC SDK Edition—refer to the *Downloading Open NFC SDK Edition* recipe.

- It's assumed that the Open NFC SDK Edition Core is already downloaded and extracted to the `NFCBook` folder in your home directory.

- The .NET framework 2.0 or later must be installed. It can be downloaded directly from Microsoft Download Center, that is, `http://www.microsoft.com/download`.

How to do it...

We are going to configure the Connection Center tool properly to recognize our virtual device as follows:

1. Open Explorer and go to the `Open NFC SDK Edition` folder.
2. Open the folder named `connection_center`.
3. Start Connection Center by right-clicking on `Connection Center.exe` and selecting `Run as administrator`.
4. The program automatically starts hidden in the taskbar. Right-click on the icon labeled Connection Center and select **Show** from the context menu.
5. Click on the **Connection** tab and configure it as shown in the following screenshot:

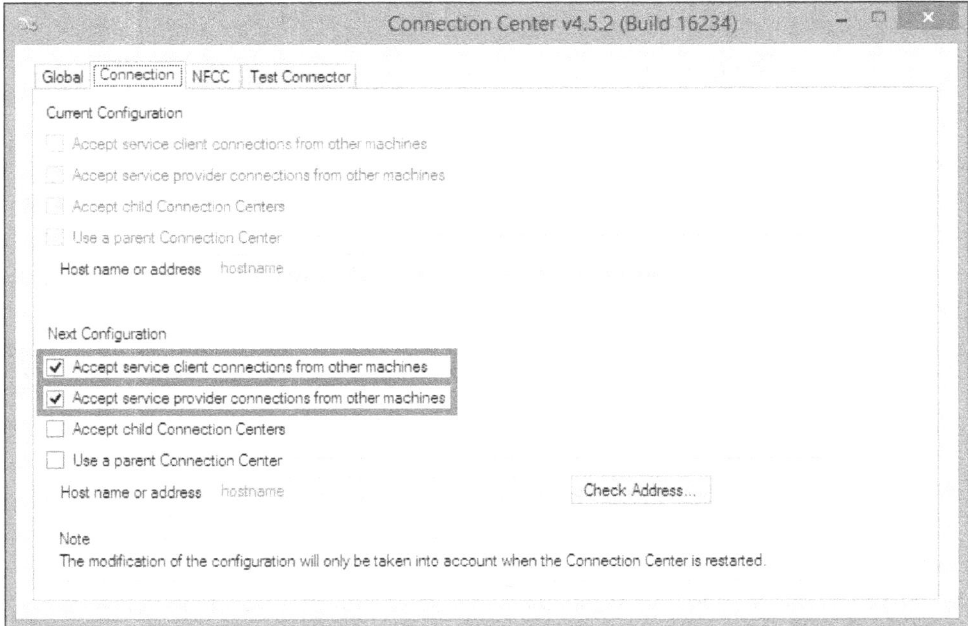

6. Restart the Connection Center tool.
7. Click on the **Connection** tab and verify whether the changes were saved.

How it works...

Since our AVD and our PC are two different machines even though the AVD is running on our PC, we need to "tell" the Connection Center tool to allow incoming and outgoing connections from other machines. This way, our AVD is able to connect to the Connection Center tool and vice versa.

> If the Windows firewall asks you to add an exception, please do so. The Connection Center tool needs to access the network.

Testing your app all together

So far, we have set up and configured several parts of the puzzle—from Open NFC Android Edition to the Simulator, passing through the AVD and the Connection Center tool.

While these puzzle pieces are very important, we can't do much with the individual pieces. So, it's time to bring them all together.

Getting ready

The following are the settings required for this recipe:

- Make sure you have downloaded Open NFC SDK Edition—refer to the *Downloading Open NFC SDK Edition* recipe

- Make sure you have properly configured the Connection Center tool—refer to the *Configuring the Connection Center tool* recipe

- Make sure you have properly configured an AVD—refer to the *Configuring an NFC-enabled testing AVD* recipe

- It's assumed that the Open NFC SDK Edition Core is located at the `NFCBook` folder in your home directory and that the Android SDK location is known

How to do it...

We'll run everything and perform a simple test to make sure everything works properly before we start our first application:

1. Start the Connection Center tool located in the Open NFC SDK Edition folder. You will receive a **Waiting for a connection...** message.

2. Start the NFC Simulator tool located in the Open NFC SDK Edition folder. In the previously started Connection Center tool, we should see a **Connected!** message as shown in the following screenshot:

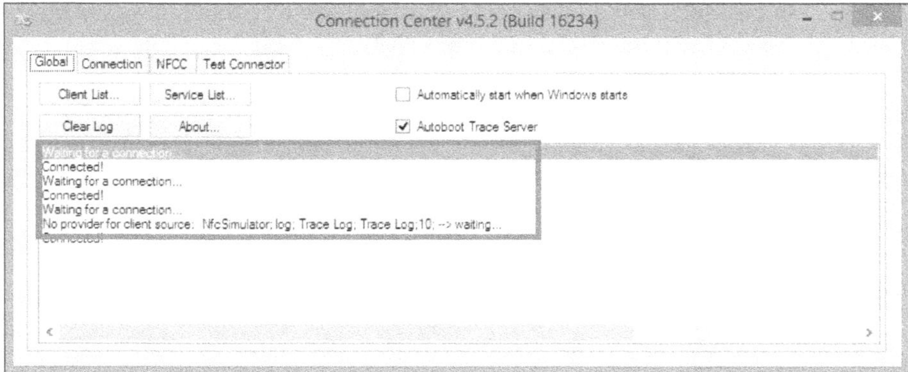

The Trace Server should be automatically started as well. We should now have the Connection Center tool, the NFC Controller Simulator, and the Trace Server running.

3. Start the previously configured AVD by clicking on **Start** in the Android Virtual Device Manager located in the Android SDK folder.

4. Once the AVD has started, we should see the following (or similar) information in the previously started tools:

    ❑   In the Connection Center tool, we should start seeing the following NFC Controller-connected messages:

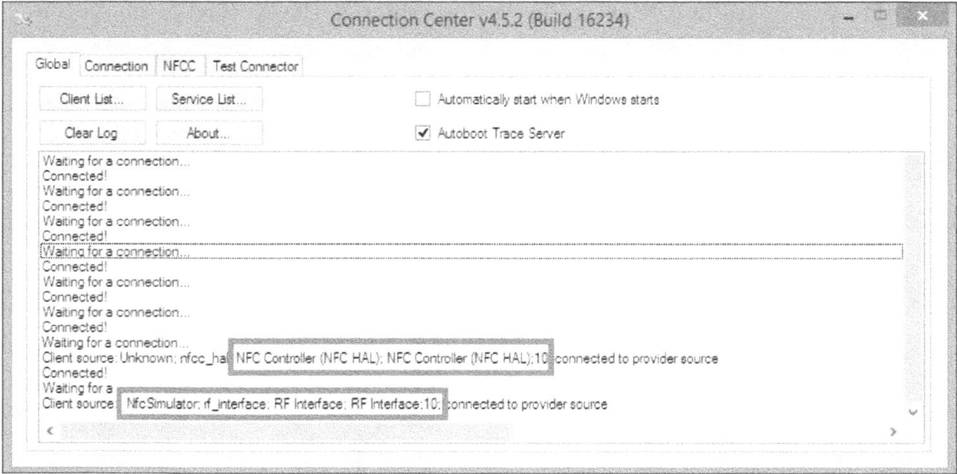

- In the Trace Server, we should start seeing a tree that shows the devices connected (on the left) and any activity in the log list, as shown in the following screenshot:

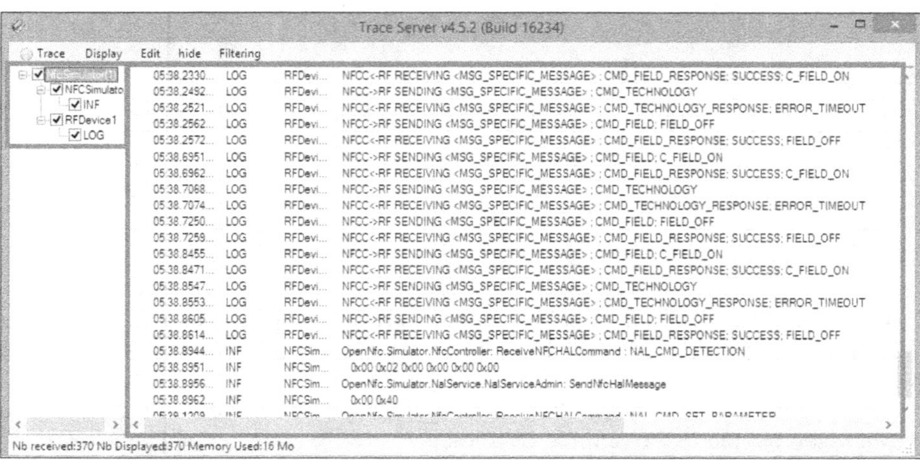

- In the NFC Controller Simulator, several orange lights should appear that indicate what communication standards the device supports, as shown in the following screenshot:

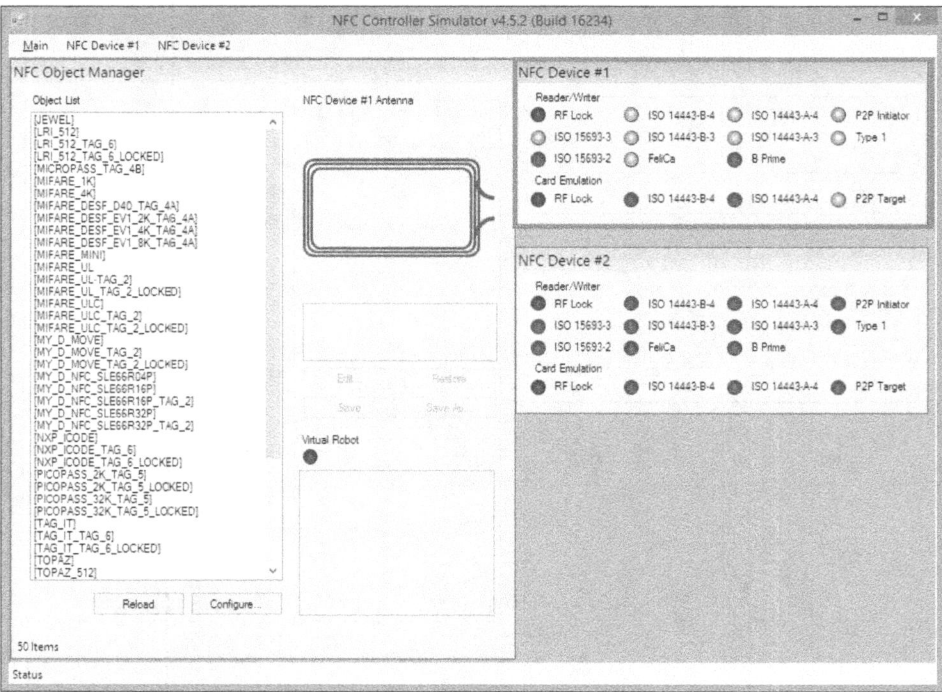

5. Now, we are going to do the final test. In the NFC Controller Simulator, double-click on **[MIREFIRE_UL_TAG2_LOCKED]** in the **Object List** panel.

    In the **NFC Device #1 Antenna** panel, a green light should appear, which means the tag was successfully dispatched to the simulator. In the simulator, the browser should be started. Now navigate to `http://www.google.com/indexToFillSomeC`, as shown in the following screenshot:

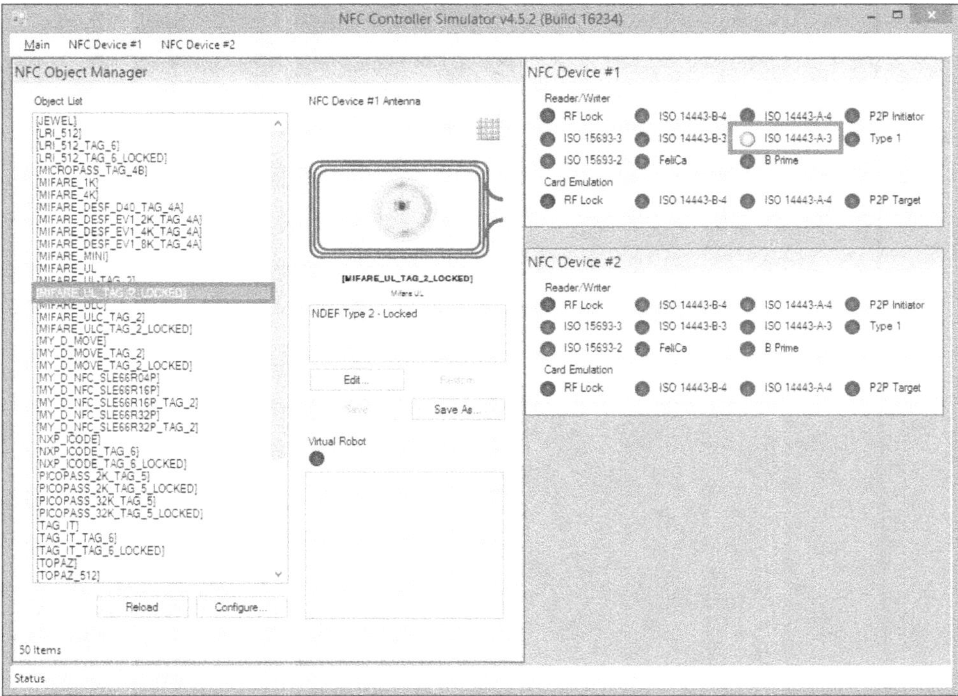

How it works...

The Connection Center tool is the first to be started. It listens for connection requests; so, when the Simulator and the AVD start, they will try to connect to a listening server. If no listener is running, nothing happens.

In the Trace Server, we can see what's happening in the communication between the devices. The sent and received messages and communications errors can be found here.

In the Simulator, we can easily see when a device is connected by looking at the top-right box. Here, we find a lot of information such as the communication standard supported by the device, represented by the orange circles, and the standard used in the last communication, represented by the green circles. The Simulator tool provides many other features such as creating custom tags. There is a detailed manual on this in the Open NFC SDK Edition Core folder.

2

Detecting a Tag

In this chapter, we will cover the following topics:

- Understanding the foreground dispatch system
- Understanding the tag dispatch system
- Verifying if your app started because of an NFC intent
- Filtering tags by their content type
- Filtering tags by their content type using programs
- Filtering tags by their technology
- Filtering tags by their technology using programs
- Filtering URI tags

Introduction

As a software developer, I have learned that one should never jump steps regarding any new subject. We should always understand how the machine works and what can we do with it. Practicing with some basic examples and some trial and error always helps setting our minds on the right path.

In this chapter, we will perform some basic examples that will allow us to start writing NFC applications and interacting with those awesome stickers called NFC tags.

NFC tags are small electronic stickers without their own power source that can be placed anywhere and contain small blocks of data—typically, URL, contacts, and text. This data can then be read by any NFC-enabled device when there is a communication between the device and the tag; this is typically done by bringing the device very close to the tag. Since the tag has no power source, we can say it is the passive element in the communication and, therefore, the active element is the NFC-enabled device such as a smartphone or an NFC reader. The tag contains an antenna that is responsible for collecting energy from the active element and powering up the chip present in the tag to establish a brief communication with the active element. All of this happens in less than a second.

The following are the several tag types that vary in reading speed, storage size, and price:

- **Tag 1 type**: This tag type is based on the ISO14443A standard; they can be read, rewritten, and set to read-only. The available size is 96 bytes but this can be expanded up to 2 KB and the communication speed is 106 kilobits/s. Broadcom Topaz is one of the tags compliant with this type.

- **Tag 2 type**: This tag type is very similar to Tag 1 type but the basic memory size is 48 bytes. A very common Tag 2 type tag is the MIFARE Ultralight.

- **Tag 3 type**: This tag type is based on the Sony FeliCa system; they can also be read, rewritten, and made read-only. The available size is 2 KB and the communication speed is 212 kilobits/s.

- **Tag 4 type**: This tag type is based on the ISO14443A/B standard, and the tags are preconfigured at the manufacturing stage and can be either read, rewritten, or read-only. The memory capacity can be up to 32 KB and the communication speed is between 106 kilobits/s and 424 kilobits/s.

There is also another well-known tag type, MIFARE Classic, that does not respect any NFC Forum specification but is still supported well on a majority of devices. Nexus 4, 5, and 7 and Galaxy S4 are examples of non-compatible devices because a different NFC hardware manufacturer was used and only tag types included in the NFC Forum specifications are compatible.

Understanding the foreground dispatch system

In Android, we can have multiple applications to complete the same task. For example, we can have multiple web browsers installed, and when we want to open a web page, the Android system prompts us to choose which application to open; NFC applications are no different. The foreground dispatch system allows an activity to intercept an NFC intent (tag detected or P2P events) and claim priority over other activities that are registered to handle the same intent. This way, when our application is in the foreground, users won't be prompted to choose which application to open, and the intent is sent to our application.

An `Intent` is a messaging object that describes an operation to be performed and is generally used to start activities, services, and facilitate data exchange among different applications.

How to do it...

We are going to create an application that demonstrates how the foreground dispatch system works and how it is useful to us. To do so, perform the following steps:

1. Open Eclipse and create a new Android application project named `NfcBookCh2Example1` with the package name `nfcbook.ch2.example1`.

2. Make sure that the `AndroidManifest.xml` file is correctly configured (refer to recipes in the previous chapter to learn how).

3. Open the `MainActivity.java` file located under `nfcbook.ch2.example1` and add the following class member:

```java
private NfcAdapter nfcAdapter;
```

4. Instantiate the `nfcAdapter` class field in the `onCreate` method:

```java
protected void onCreate(Bundle savedInstanceState) {

    ...

    nfcAdapter = NfcAdapter.getDefaultAdapter(this);
}
```

5. Override the `onNewIntent` method and insert the following code:

```java
@Override
protected void onNewIntent(Intent intent) {

    Toast.makeText(this, "NFC intent received", Toast.LENGTH_SHORT).
show();

    super.onNewIntent(intent);
}
```

6. Override the `onResume` method and insert the following code:

```java
@Override
protected void onResume() {
    super.onResume();

    Intent intent = new Intent(this, MainActivity.class).
addFlags(Intent.FLAG_RECEIVER_REPLACE_PENDING);

    PendingIntent pendingIntent = PendingIntent.getActivity(this, 0,
intent, 0);
```

```java
IntentFilter[] intentFilter = new IntentFilter[] { };

nfcAdapter.enableForegroundDispatch(this, pendingIntent,
intentFilter, null);
}
```

7. Override the `onPause` method and insert the following code:

```java
@Override
protected void onPause() {
  super.onPause();

  nfcAdapter.disableForegroundDispatch(this);
}
```

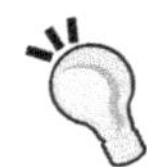

If you are having problems knowing which classes to import, you can let Eclipse do that for you by going to the **Source** menu and selecting the **Organize Imports** option.

How it works...

When the activity starts, the `onResume` method is called. Then, we enable the foreground dispatch system on the NFC adapter, which indicates that any `Intent` should be dispatched to our `MainActivity` file. When the activity receives an incoming intent, the `onNewIntent` method gets called, so we need to override it and implement our code. When the user leaves the application or the device enters sleep mode, the `onPause` method gets called, which means that the app is no longer in active use; so, it's a good practice to disable the foreground dispatch system or unexpected behaviors can occur. If the user gets back to the application, the `onResume` method gets called again, and with that, the foreground dispatch system is started again.

We create a `PendingIntent` object so that the Android system can populate it with the tag details and use the `IntentFilter` object to let the foreground dispatch system know what intent we want to intercept. If the intent doesn't match our required filters, the foreground dispatch system will fall back to the intent dispatch system.

Avoid getting that horrible **App has stopped** message by testing whether the `NfcAdapter` instance is available and enabled, every time.

Understanding the tag dispatch system

The Android system has a structured way to deal with the different tag types, technologies, and content. In this recipe, we will create a simple app that will allow us to visualize the implemented structure.

How to do it...

By performing the following steps, we are going to create an application that will allow us to see the triggered action when we tag different tags in our device:

1. Open the `MainActivity.java` file from the previously created `NfcBookCh2Example1` project.

2. On the `onNewIntent` method, add the following lines of code:

```
String action = intent.getAction();
Toast.makeText(this, action, Toast.LENGTH_SHORT).show();
```

3. Open the NFC Simulator tool and simulate a few taps for different tag types and then see the results.

   In the NFC Simulator tool, when tag names end with `_LOCKED`, it means that the tags are formatted and have content on them; probably, an NDEF record. Therefore, the `NDEF_DISCOVERED` action will be triggered. Unformatted tags will trigger the `TAG_DISCOVERED` action.

How it works...

Android's dispatch system has three main events for NFC tag detection:

- `NDEF_DISCOVERED`: This event is triggered when a tag that contains an `Ndef` record is detected.

- `TECH_DISCOVERED`: This event is triggered for unmapped or `Ndef` tags that have not been formatted.

- `TAG_DISCOVERED`: This event is triggered when no activity is registered to handle the previous actions. Note that this intent is a leftover from API level 9, and we should use the `TECH_DISCOVERED` event instead.

In this example, we don't specify which action we handle, so we receive all three. Depending on the tag type and content we use to test, the toast shown will change.

Verifying if your app started because of an NFC intent

Because the `onNewIntent` method is triggered by any intent, we need to perform some additional tests just to make sure it is an NFC intent.

How to do it...

1. Open the `MainActivity.java` file from the previously created `NfcBookCh2Example1` project.

2. In the `onNewIntent` method, add the following lines of code:

```
if (!intent.hasExtra(NfcAdapter.EXTRA_TAG)) {
  return;
}
```

How it works...

On the `onNewIntent` method, we test the incoming intent for its action. The intent action must match `ACTION_NDEF_DISCOVERED`, `ACTION_TAG_DISCOVERED`, or `ACTION_TECH_DISCOVERED`, to be an NFC intent. In this example, we are only testing for the `ACTION_NDEF_DISCOVERED` action because this is the simplest format to work with.

When the `Intent` action is an NDEF, `EXTRA_TAG` is required so that we can test if the extra is not null. This extra represents the tag object instance.

For more readable and organized code, we can create a method that verifies if any intent is an NFC intent, as shown in the following code:

```
boolean isNfcIntent(Intent intent) {
    return intent.hasExtra(NfcAdapter.EXTRA_TAG);
}

@Override
protected void onNewIntent(Intent intent) {

    if ( isNfcIntent(intent) ) {

        ...

    }
}
```

Filtering tags by their content type

NFC tags can hold several types of data such as URIs and simple text. In our applications, we may only want to handle tags in which content is recognized. That way, we avoid unexpected exceptions.

How to do it...

We'll create an application that is executed only when the content type matches what is specified by us. Open the `AndroidManifest.xml` file from the previously created `NfcBookCh2Example1` project and add the following `intent-filter` to the main activity declaration:

```xml
<intent-filter>
    <action android:name="android.nfc.action.NDEF_DISCOVERED"/>
    <category android:name="android.intent.category.DEFAULT"/>
    <data android:mimeType="text/plain" />
</intent-filter>
```

How it works...

While declaring the activity in the `AndroidManifest.xml` file, we also specify that the activity only receives intents that match some conditions. In this case, the main activity receives only NFC intents with the `text/plain` data. The checking of the intent type should not be removed from the `onNewIntent` method since we are still able to send other intent types to the `MainActivity.java` file.

We can specify other mime types, such as a custom type, or in the case of a URL, we can specify its parts such as the schema:

```
<intent-filter>
    <action android:name="android.nfc.action.NDEF_
DISCOVERED" />
    <category android:name="android.intent.category.
DEFAULT" />
    <data android:mimeType="application/vnd.nfcbook.
example2ch2" />
</intent-filter>


<intent-filter>
    <action android:name="android.nfc.action.NDEF_
DISCOVERED" />
    <category android:name="android.intent.category.
DEFAULT" />
    <data android:scheme="https" />
</intent-filter>
```

NFC Forum external types are filtered as shown in the following code:

```
<intent-filter>
    <action android:name="android.nfc.action.NDEF_
DISCOVERED" />
    <category android:name="android.intent.category.
DEFAULT" />
    <data android:scheme="vnd.android.nfc"
        android:host="ext"
        android:pathPrefix="/com.
myexternaltype:externalType"/>
</intent-filter>
```

Filtering tags by their content type programmatically

NFC tags can hold several types of data commonly used in several applications. In our applications, we may only want to handle tags in which the content is recognized. That way, we avoid unexpected exceptions and messing up with other developers' applications.

How to do it...

By performing the following steps, we will programmatically define the tag-content filter in which the application gets executed:

1. Open Eclipse and create a new Android application project named `NfcBookCh2Example2` with the package name `nfcbook.ch2.example2`.

2. Open the `MainActivity.java` file located under `nfcbook.ch2.example2` and add the following class member:

   ```
   private NfcAdapter nfcAdapter;.
   ```

3. Instantiate the `nfcAdapter` class field in the `onCreate` method:

   ```
   protected void onCreate(Bundle savedInstanceState) {

   ...

   nfcAdapter = NfcAdapter.getDefaultAdapter(this);
   }
   ```

4. Implement the following method and invoke it in the `onResume` method, as shown in the following code:

   ```
   void enableForegroundDispatch() {

     Intent intent = new Intent(getApplicationContext(),
   MainActivity.class)
         .addFlags(Intent.FLAG_RECEIVER_REPLACE_PENDING);

     PendingIntent pendingIntent = PendingIntent.getActivity(
         getApplicationContext(), 0, intent, 0);

     IntentFilter intentFilter = new IntentFilter(
         NfcAdapter.ACTION_NDEF_DISCOVERED);

     intentFilter.addDataScheme("https");

     if (nfcAdapter != null)
       nfcAdapter.enableForegroundDispatch(this, pendingIntent,
           new IntentFilter[] { intentFilter }, null);
   }
   ```

5. Implement the `isNfcIntent` method:

   ```
   boolean isNfcIntent(Intent intent) {
   return intent.hasExtra(NfcAdapter.EXTRA_TAG);
   }
   ```

6. Override the `onNewIntent` method and insert the following code:

```
@Override
protected void onNewIntent(Intent intent) {

    if ( isNfcIntent(intent) ) {

        Toast.makeText( this, "NFC intent received",
            Toast.LENGTH_SHORT).show();

    }
}
```

7. Override the `onPause` method and insert the following code:

```
@Override
protected void onPause() {
super.onPause();
nfcAdapter.disableForegroundDispatch(this);
}
```

How it works...

We are filtering the intents with the conditions added in the `IntentFilter` class passed to the `enableForegroundDispatch` method. In the `onNewIntent` method, we handle all intents dispatched to our activity. This code checks if the new intent is an NFC intent. We can also verify this by testing for the intent type, which will return its MIME type.

Filtering tags by their technology

There are several types of NFC tags. They mostly differ on the storage capacity and on the communication standard used. In our application, we may want to use only a specific type of tag because of a certain characteristic of that specific tag. The Android SDK supports the most frequent tag types such as MIFARE Classic and MIFARE Ultralight tags.

How to do it...

We will create an application that is executed only when the tag technology matches the one specified by us:

1. Open Eclipse and create a new Android application project named `NfcBookCh2Example3` with the package name `nfcbook.ch2.example3`.

2. Open the `MainActivity.java` file, override the `onNewIntent` method, and insert the following code:

```java
@Override
protected void onNewIntent(Intent intent) {

  if ( isNfcIntent(intent) ) {

    Toast.makeText( this, "NFC intent received", Toast.LENGTH_
SHORT).show();

  }
}
```

3. Implement the `isNfcIntent` method:

```java
boolean isNfcIntent(Intent intent) {
return intent.hasExtra(NfcAdapter.EXTRA_TAG);
}
```

4. In the project tree, create a folder named `xml` under the `res` folder.

5. In the `xml` folder we just created, create an XML file named `nfc_tech_filter.xml`.

6. Add the following code to the `nfc_tech_filder.xml` file:

```xml
<resources xmlns:xliff="urn:oasis:names:tc:xliff:document:1.2">
    <tech-list>
        <tech>android.nfc.tech.NfcA</tech>
    </tech-list>
  <tech-list>
        <tech>android.nfc.tech.MifareClassic</tech>
    </tech-list>
</resources>
```

7. Open the `AndroidManifest.xml` file and add the following `intent-filter` to the main activity declaration:

```xml
<intent-filter>
    <action android:name="android.nfc.action.TECH_DISCOVERED"/>
</intent-filter>

<meta-data android:name="android.nfc.action.TECH_DISCOVERED"
    android:resource="@xml/nfc_tech_filter" />
```

How it works...

In the `onNewIntent` method, we handle all intents dispatched to our activity. This code checks to see if the new intent is an NFC intent. We can also verify this by testing to see if any of the listed tag objects are available in our tag tech list.

Filtering tags by their technology using programs

There are several types of NFC tags. They mostly differ on the storage capacity and on the communication standard used. In our application, we may want to use only a specific type of tag because of a certain characteristic of that specific tag. The Android SDK supports the most frequent tag types such as MIFARE Classic and MIFARE Ultralight tags.

How to do it...

By performing the following steps, we will create an application that is executed only when the programmatically defined technology filters match the ones specified by us:

1. Open Eclipse and create a new Android application project named `NfcBookCh2Example4` with the package name `nfcbook.ch2.example4`.

2. Open `MainActivity.java` located under `nfcbook.ch2.example4`, implement the following method, and invoke it in the `onResume` method:

```
void enableForegroundDispatch() {

    Intent intent = new Intent(this, MainActivity.class).
ddFlags(Intent.FLAG_RECEIVER_REPLACE_PENDING);

    PendingIntent pendingIntent = PendingIntent.getActivity(this,
0, intent, 0);

    String[][] techList = new String[][] { { android.nfc.tech.NfcA.
class.getName(), android.nfc.tech.IsoDep.class.getName() } };

    nfcAdapter.enableForegroundDispatch(this, pendingIntent, null,
techList);

}
```

3. Override the `onNewIntent` method and insert the following code:

```
@Override
protected void onNewIntent(Intent intent) {
```

```
    if (isNfcIntent(intent)) {

        Toast.makeText(this, "NFC intent received", Toast.LENGTH_
    SHORT).show();

    }
    super.onNewIntent(intent);
}
```

4. Add the following class member and instantiate it in the `onCreate` method:

```
private NfcAdapter nfcAdapter;

protected void onCreate(Bundle savedInstanceState) {
...
nfcAdapter = NfcAdapter.getDefaultAdapter(this);
}
```

5. Implement the `isNfcIntent` method:

```
boolean isNfcIntent(Intent intent) {
return intent.hasExtra(NfcAdapter.EXTRA_TAG);
}
```

How it works...

In this recipe, we used the foreground dispatch system to filter intents by their technology. The last parameter of the `enableForegroundDispatch` method is a `String[][]` that contains the tech class names we want to filter.

Please note that the OpenNfc simulator does not work properly when filtering tags by technology so, this recipe should be ideally tested with a real device.

Filtering URI tags

Filtering activities in the `AndroidManifest.xml` file can really simplify our work and it allows us to define a more advanced filter than just the content type of a tag. In this recipe, we will learn how we can filter a URI tag.

How to do it...

By performing the following steps, we will create an application that is executed only when the URI parts present in the tags match our filters:

1. Open Eclipse and create a new Android application project named `NfcBookCh2Example5` with the package name `nfcbook.ch2.example5`.

2. Open `MainActivity`, override the `onNewIntent` method, and insert the following code:

```java
@Override
protected void onNewIntent(Intent intent) {

   if ( isNfcIntent(intent) ) {

      Toast.makeText( this, "NFC intent received", Toast.LENGTH_
SHORT).show();

   }
   super.onNewIntent(intent);
}
```

3. Implement the `isNfcIntent` method:

```java
boolean isNfcIntent(Intent intent) {
return intent.hasExtra(NfcAdapter.EXTRA_TAG);
}
```

4. Open the `AndroidManifest.xml` file and add the following `intent-filter` to the main activity declaration:

```xml
<intent-filter>
    <action android:name="android.nfc.action.NDEF_DISCOVERED" />
    <category android:name="android.intent.category.DEFAULT" />
    <data android:scheme="http"
            android:host="packtpub.com" />
</intent-filter>
```

How it works...

While declaring the activity in the `AndroidManifest.xml` file, we also specify that the activity only receives intents that match some conditions. In this case, the main activity only receives NFC intents where the URL protocol matches `http` and the host, `packtpub.com`. If we have several filters defined for one activity, only the most accurate filter will match and launch an application.

> Besides the scheme and the host, we can even specify the path:
>
> ```xml
> <intent-filter>
>     <action android:name="android.nfc.action.NDEF_
> DISCOVERED" />
>     <category android:name="android.intent.category.
> DEFAULT" />
>     <data android:scheme="http"
>             android:host="packtpub.com"
>                 android:pathPrefix="/index.php" />
> </intent-filter>
> ```

3

Writing Tag Content

In this chapter, we will cover the following topics:

- Working with the NDEF record
- Writing a URI-formatted record
- Writing a text-formatted record
- Using Android Application Record
- Working with external types
- Working with custom mimes

Introduction

As we saw in the previous chapters, the NFC Forum is responsible for developing standards-based NFC specifications to allow interoperability between different devices and tags. One of the specifications created by the NFC Forum is **NFC Data Exchange Format** (**NDEF**). The NDEF specification defines the message encapsulation format to exchange information between two NFC-enabled devices or devices with the NFC tag. NDEF is a lightweight, binary message format that can be used to encapsulate several custom payloads. Using this abstraction layer allows us to create the standard tag content compatible with all the NFC Forum tag types, ignoring the fact that each tag type has different hardware setups and memory layouts.

The NDEF Message is composed by one or more NDEF records, and each record contains the payload and a header in which the data length and type and identifier are stored.

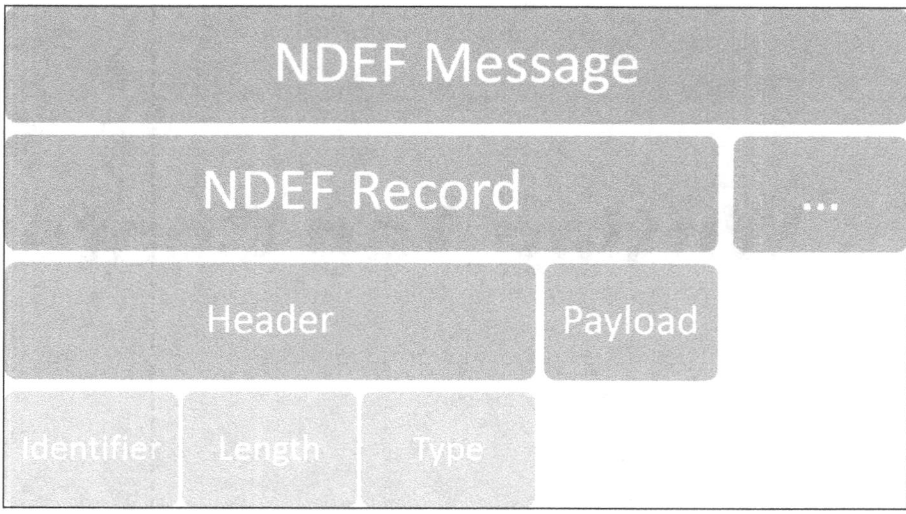

In this chapter, we will create some examples that will allow us to work with the NDEF standard and start writing NFC applications.

Working with the NDEF record

Android provides an easy way to read and write data when it is formatted as per the standard NDEF. This format is the easiest way for us to work with tag data because it saves us from performing lots of operations and processes of reading and writing raw bytes. So, unless we need to get our hands dirty and write our own protocol, this is the way to go (you can still build it on top of NDEF and achieve a custom, yet standard-based protocol).

Getting ready

- Make sure you have a working Android development environment. If you don't, ADT Bundle is a good environment to start with (you can access it by navigating to `http://developer.android.com/sdk/index.html`).

- Make sure you have an NFC-enabled Android device or a virtual test environment; refer to the *Testing your app all together* recipe from *Chapter 1, Getting Started with NFC*.

- It will be assumed that Eclipse is the development IDE.

How to do it...

We are going to create an application that writes any NDEF record to a tag by performing the following steps:

1. Open Eclipse and create a new Android application project named `NfcBookCh3Example1` with the package name `nfcbook.ch3.example1`.

2. Make sure the `AndroidManifest.xml` file is correctly configured (refer to the *Requesting NFC permissions* recipe from *Chapter 1, Getting Started with NFC*).

3. Open the `MainActivity.java` file located under `com.nfcbook.ch3.example1` and add the following class member:

   ```
   private NfcAdapter nfcAdapter;
   ```

4. Implement the `enableForegroundDispatch` method and filter tags by using `Ndef` and `NdefFormatable`. `Invoke` in the `onResume` method:

   ```
   private void enableForegroundDispatch() {
   Intent intent = new Intent(this, MainActivity.class).
   addFlags(Intent.FLAG_RECEIVER_REPLACE_PENDING);

     PendingIntent pendingIntent =
       PendingIntent.getActivity(this, 0, intent, 0);

     IntentFilter[] intentFilter = new IntentFilter[] {};

     String[][] techList = new String[][] { { android.nfc.tech.
   Ndef.class.getName() }, { android.nfc.tech.NdefFormatable.class.
   getName() } };
   if ( Build.DEVICE.matches(".*generic.*") ) {
    //clean up the tech filter when in emulator since it doesn't work
   properly.
    techList = null;
   }
     nfcAdapter.enableForegroundDispatch(this, pendingIntent,
       intentFilter, techList);
   }
   ```

5. Instantiate the `nfcAdapter` class field in the `onCreate` method:

   ```
   protected void onCreate(Bundle savedInstanceState) {
   ...
   nfcAdapter = NfcAdapter.getDefaultAdapter(this);
   }
   ```

6. Implement the `formatTag` method:

```java
private boolean formatTag(Tag tag, NdefMessage ndefMessage) {

    try {

        NdefFormatable ndefFormat = NdefFormatable.get(tag);

        if (ndefFormat != null) {
            ndefFormat.connect();
            ndefFormat.format(ndefMessage);
            ndefFormat.close();
            return true;
        }

    } catch (Exception e) {
        Log.e("formatTag", e.getMessage());
    }

    return false;
}
```

7. Implement the `writeNdefMessage` method:

```java
private boolean writeNdefMessage(Tag tag, NdefMessage
    ndefMessage) {
    try {

        if (tag != null) {

            Ndef ndef = Ndef.get(tag);
            if (ndef == null) {
                return formatTag(tag, ndefMessage);
            } else {
            ndef.connect();

                if (ndef.isWritable()) {
                    ndef.writeNdefMessage(ndefMessage);

                    ndef.close();
                    return true;
                }

                ndef.close();
            }
        }
```

```java
    } catch (Exception e) {
      Log.e("formatTag", e.getMessage());
    }


    return false;
}
```

8. Implement the `isNfcIntent` method:

```java
boolean isNfcIntent(Intent intent) {
    return intent.hasExtra(NfcAdapter.EXTRA_TAG);

}
```

9. Override the `onNewIntent` method using the following code:

```java
@Override
protected void onNewIntent(Intent intent) {

    try {
      if (isNfcIntent(intent)) {

        NdefRecord ndefEmptyRecord = new
          NdefRecord(NdefRecord.TNF_EMPTY, new byte[]{}, new byte[]
            {}, new byte[]{});

        NdefMessage ndefMessage = new NdefMessage(new
          NdefRecord[] { ndefEmptyRecord });

        Tag tag =
          intent.getParcelableExtra(NfcAdapter.EXTRA_TAG);

        if (writeNdefMessage(tag, ndefMessage)) {
          Toast.makeText(this, "Tag written!",
            Toast.LENGTH_SHORT).show();
        } else {
          Toast.makeText(this, "Failed to write tag",
            Toast.LENGTH_SHORT).show();
        }
      }

    } catch (Exception e) {
      Log.e("onNewIntent", e.getMessage());
    }


}
```

10. Override the `onPause` method and insert the following code:

```
@Override
protected void onPause() {
super.onPause();
nfcAdapter.disableForegroundDispatch(this);
}
```

11. Open the NFC Simulator tool and simulate a few tags. The tag should be marked as modified, as shown in the following screenshot:

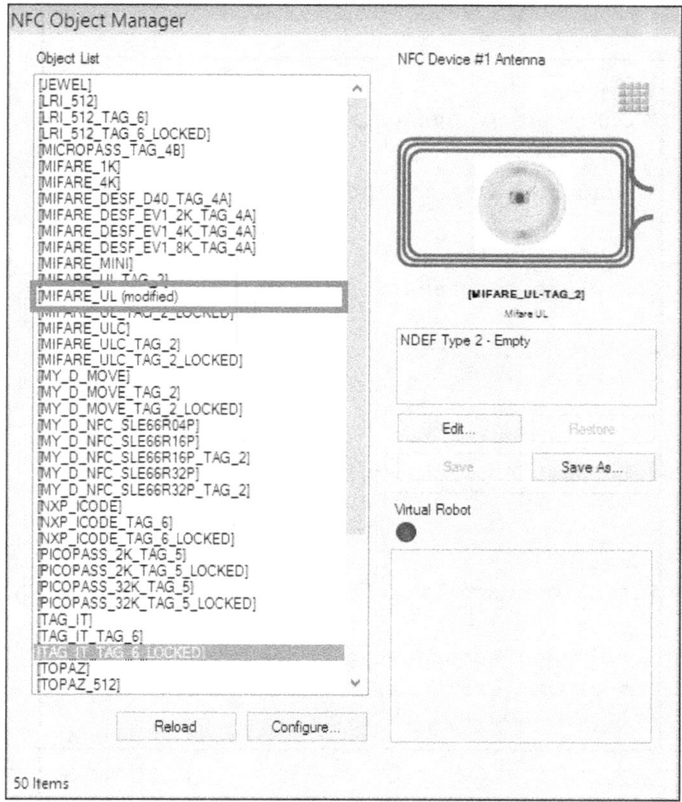

In the NFC Simulator, a tag name that ends with **_LOCKED** is not writable, so we won't be able to write any content to the tag and, therefore, a **Failed to write tag** toast will appear.

How it works...

NFC intents carry an extra value with them that is a virtual representation of the tag and can be obtained using the `NfcAdapter.EXTRA_TAG` key. We can get information about the tag, such as the tag ID and its content type, through this object.

In the `onNewIntent` method, we retrieve the tag instance and then use other classes provided by Android to easily read, write, and retrieve even more information about the tag. These classes are as follows:

- `android.nfc.tech.Ndef`: This class provides methods to retrieve and modify the `NdefMessage` object on a tag

- `android.nfc.tech.NdefFormatable`: This class provides methods to format tags that are capable of being formatted as NDEF

The first thing we need to do while writing a tag is to call the `get(Tag tag)` method from the `Ndef` class, which will return an instance of the same class. Then, we need to open a connection with the tag by calling the `connect()` method. With an open connection, we can now write a NDEF message to the tag by calling the `writeNdefMessage(NdefMessage msg)` method. Checking whether the tag is writable or not is always a good practice to prevent unwanted exceptions. We can do this by calling the `isWritable()` method. Note that this method may not account for physical write protection. When everything is done, we call the `close()` method to release the previously opened connection.

If the `get(Tag tag)` method returns null, it means that the tag is not formatted as per the NDEF format, and we should try to format it correctly.

For formatting a tag with the NDEF format, we use the `NdefFormatable` class in the same way as we did with the `Ndef` class. However, in this case, we want to format the tag and write a message. This is achieved by calling the `format(NdefMessage firstMessage)` method. So, we should call the `get(Tag tag)` method, then open a connection by calling `connect()`, format the tag, and write the message by calling the `format(NdefMessage firstMessage)` method. Finally, close the connection with the `close()` method.

If the `get(Tag tag)` method returns null, it means that the tag is the Android NFC API that cannot automatically format the tag to NDEF.

An NDEF message is composed of several NDEF records. Each of these records is composed of four key properties:

- **Type Name Format (TNF)**: This property defines how the type field should be interpreted
- **Record Type Definition (RTD)**: This property is used together with the TNF to help Android create the correct NDEF message and trigger the corresponding intent
- **Id**: This property lets you define a custom identifier for the record
- **Payload**: This property contains the content that will be transported to the record

Using the combinations between the TNF and the RTD, we can create several different NDEF records to hold our data and even create our custom types. In this recipe, we created an empty record.

The main TNF property values of a record are as follows:

- `- TNF_ABSOLUTE_URI`: This is a URI-type field
- `- TNF_WELL_KNOWN`: This is an NFC Forum-defined URN
- `- TNF_EXTERNAL_TYPE`: This is a URN-type field
- `- TNF_MIME_MEDIA`: This is a MIME type based on the type specified

The main RTF property values of a record are:

- `- RTD_URI`: This is the URI based on the payload
- `- RTD_TEXT`: This is the NFC Forum-defined record type

Writing a URI-formatted record

URI is probably the most common content written to NFC tags. It allows you to share a website, an online service, or a link to the online content. This can be used, for example, in advertising and marketing.

How to do it...

We are going to create an application that writes URI records to a tag by performing the following steps. The URI will be hardcoded and will point to the Packt Publishing website.

1. Open Eclipse and create a new Android application project named `NfcBookCh3Example2`.

2. Make sure the `AndroidManifest.xml` file is configured correctly (refer to the *Requesting NFC permissions* recipe from *Chapter 1, Getting Started with NFC*).

3. Set the minimum SDK version to `14`:

   ```
   <uses-sdk android:minSdkVersion="14" />
   ```

4. Implement the `enableForegroundDispatch`, `isNfcIntent`, `formatTag`, and `writeNdefMessage` methods from the previous recipe—steps 2, 4, 6, and 7.

5. Add the following class member and instantiate it in the onCreate method:

   ```
   private NfcAdapter nfcAdapter;

   protected void onCreate(Bundle savedInstanceState) {
   ...
   nfcAdapter = NfcAdapter.getDefaultAdapter(this);
   }
   ```

6. Override the `onNewIntent` method and place the following code:

   ```
   @Override
   protected void onNewIntent(Intent intent) {

     try {

       if (isNfcIntent(intent)) {

         NdefRecord uriRecord = NdefRecord.createUri
           ("http://www.packtpub.com");

         NdefMessage ndefMessage = new NdefMessage(new
           NdefRecord[] { uriRecord });

         Tag tag =
           intent.getParcelableExtra(NfcAdapter.EXTRA_TAG);

         boolean writeResult = writeNdefMessage(tag,
           ndefMessage);

         if (writeResult) {
         Toast.makeText(this, "Tag written!",
           Toast.LENGTH_SHORT).show();
         } else {
   ```

```
            Toast.makeText(this, "Tag write failed!",
              Toast.LENGTH_SHORT).show();
          }
        }
      } catch (Exception e) {
        Log.e("onNewIntent", e.getMessage());
      }

      super.onNewIntent(intent);
    }
```

7. Run the application.

8. Tap a tag on your phone or simulate a tap in the NFC Simulator. A **Write Successful!** toast should appear.

How it works...

URIs are perfect content for NFC tags because with a relatively small amount of content, we can send users to more rich and complete resources. These types of records are the most easy to create, and this is done by calling the `NdefRecord.createUri` method and passing the URI as the first parameter.

URIs are not necessarily URLs for a website. We can use other URIs that are quite well-known in Android such as the following:

```
- tel:+000 000 000 000
- sms:+000 000 000 000
```

If we write the `tel:` uri syntax, the user will be prompted to initiate a phone call.

We can always create a URI record the hard way without using the `createUri` method:

```
public NdefRecord createUriRecord(String uri) {
  NdefRecord rtdUriRecord = null;
  try {
    byte[] uriField;
    uriField = uri.getBytes("UTF-8");
    byte[] payload = new byte[uriField.length + 1]; //+1 for the URI
prefix
      payload[0] = 0x00; //prefixes the URI
    System.arraycopy(uriField, 0, payload, 1, uriField.length);
    rtdUriRecord = new NdefRecord(NdefRecord.TNF_WELL_KNOWN,
NdefRecord.RTD_URI, new byte[0], payload);
    } catch (UnsupportedEncodingException e) {
```

```
        Log.e("createUriRecord", e.getMessage());
    }
    return rtdUriRecord;
}
```

The first byte in the payload indicates which prefix should be used with the URI. This way, we don't need to write the whole URI in the tag, which saves some tag space.

The following list describes the recognized prefixes:

```
0x00      No prepending is done
0x01      http://www.
0x02      https://www.
0x03      http://
0x04      https://
0x05      tel:
0x06      mailto:
0x07      ftp://anonymous:anonymous@
0x08      ftp://ftp.
0x09      ftps://
0x0A      sftp://
0x0B      smb://
0x0C      nfs://
0x0D      ftp://
0x0E      dav://
0x0F      news:
0x10      telnet://
0x11      imap:
0x12      rtsp://
0x13      urn:
0x14      pop:
0x15      sip:
0x16      sips:
0x17      tftp:
0x18      btspp://
0x19      btl2cap://
0x1A      btgoep://
0x1B      tcpobex://
0x1C      irdaobex://
0x1D      file://
0x1E      urn:epc:id:
0x1F      urn:epc:tag:
0x20      urn:epc:pat:
0x21      urn:epc:raw:
0x22      urn:epc:
0x23      urn:nfc:
```

Writing a text-formatted record

As we saw in the *Working with the NDEF record* recipe, we can write different tag content formats. In this recipe, we will see how to store text in a tag.

How to do it...

We are going to create an application that creates and writes a text-formatted record to a tag:

1. Open Eclipse and create a new Android application project named `NfcBookCh3Example3` with the package name `nfcbook.ch3.example3`.

2. Make sure the `AndroidManifest.xml` file is configured correctly (refer to the *Requesting NFC permissions* recipe from *Chapter 1, Getting Started with NFC*).

3. Make sure the foreground dispatch system is enabled (refer to the *Understanding the foreground dispatch system* recipe from *Chapter 2, Detecting a Tag*).

4. Open the `MainActivity.java` file located under `nfcbook.ch3.example3` and add the following class member:

   ```java
   private NfcAdapter nfcAdapter;
   ```

5. Instantiate the `nfcAdapter` class field in the `onCreate` method:

   ```java
   protected void onCreate(Bundle savedInstanceState) {
   ...
   nfcAdapter = NfcAdapter.getDefaultAdapter(this);
   }
   ```

6. Implement the `createTextRecord` method, as shown in the following code:

   ```java
   public NdefRecord createTextRecord(String content) {

     try {

       byte[] language;
       language = Locale.getDefault().getLanguage().
   getBytes("UTF-8");

       final byte[] text = content.getBytes("UTF-8");

       final int languageSize = language.length;
       final int textLength = text.length;

       final ByteArrayOutputStream payload = new
         ByteArrayOutputStream(1 + languageSize + textLength);
   ```

```java
        payload.write((byte) (languageSize & 0x1F));
        payload.write(language, 0, languageSize);
        payload.write(text, 0, textLength);

        return new NdefRecord(NdefRecord.TNF_WELL_KNOWN,
          NdefRecord.RTD_TEXT, new byte[0], payload.toByteArray());
    } catch (UnsupportedEncodingException e) {
      Log.e("createTextRecord", e.getMessage());
    }

    return null;
}
```

7. Implement the `isNfcIntent`, `formatTag`, and `writeNdefMessage` methods from step 7 of the previous recipe.

8. Override the `onNewIntent` method and place the following code:

```java
@Override
protected void onNewIntent(Intent intent) {

  try {

    if (isNfcIntent(intent)) {

      NdefRecord ndefRecord = createTextRecord("My string
content");
      NdefMessage ndefMessage = new NdefMessage(new NdefRecord[] {
ndefRecord });

      Tag tag = intent.getParcelableExtra(NfcAdapter.EXTRA_TAG);

      boolean writeResult = writeNdefMessage(tag, ndefMessage);

      if (writeResult) {
        Toast.makeText(this, "Tag written!", Toast.LENGTH_SHORT).
show();
      } else {
        Toast.makeText(this, "Tag write failed!", Toast.LENGTH_
SHORT).show();
      }
    }

  } catch (Exception e) {
    Log.e("onNewIntent", e.getMessage());
  }


}
```

9.   Run the application.

10. Tap a tag or simulate a tap in the NFC Simulator.

11. A **Write Successful!** toast should appear.

How it works...

Writing a string to a tag is a little tricky because the payload doesn't directly correspond to the text that we write. The payload sent to the tag is a byte concatenation that contains the language of the string, the string itself, and an additional byte—the first one—which is a bitwise AND operator on the language size (to indicate the character encoding used). This is done on the `createTextRecord` method.

When we read text from a tag, we need to perform the inverse operation and get the string language and the string itself from the byte array.

In this recipe, we used the system's default language to format our string, but we can use any other language independent of the user's language.

Using Android Application Record

When we develop an app to write and read NFC tags, we most probably want this to happen when the user taps on a tag on their phone, and our app starts automatically even if it isn't running in the foreground. The Android system provides us with a pretty simple solution for this—AAR.

How to do it...

We are going to create an application that creates and writes an AAR to a tag by performing the following steps:

1.   Open Eclipse and create a new Android application project named `NfcBookCh3Example4` with the package name `nfcbook.ch3.example4`.

2.   Make sure the `AndroidManifest.xml` file is configured correctly (refer to the *Requesting NFC permissions* recipe of *Chapter 1, Getting Started with NFC*).

3.   Set the minimum SDK version to 14:

```
<uses-sdk android:minSdkVersion="14" />
```

4.   Make sure the foreground dispatch system is enabled (refer to the *Understanding the foreground dispatch system* recipe in *Chapter 2, Detecting a Tag*).

5.   Open `MainActivity` located under `nfcbook.ch3.example4` and add the following class member:

```
private NfcAdapter nfcAdapter;
```

6. Instantiate the `nfcAdapter` class field in the `onCreate` method:

```java
protected void onCreate(Bundle savedInstanceState) {
...
nfcAdapter = NfcAdapter.getDefaultAdapter(this);
}
```

7. Implement the `isNfcIntent`, `formatTag`, and `writeNdefMessage` methods from the previous recipe-step 7.

8. Override the `onNewIntent` method and add the following code:

```java
@Override
protected void onNewIntent(Intent intent) {

  try {
    if (isNfcIntent(intent)) {

      NdefRecord aaRecord = NdefRecord.
createApplicationRecord(this.getPackageName());
      NdefMessage ndefMessage = new NdefMessage(new NdefRecord[] {
aaRecord });

      Tag tag = intent.getParcelableExtra(NfcAdapter.EXTRA_TAG);

      boolean writeResult = writeNdefMessage(tag, ndefMessage);
      if (writeResult) {
        Toast.makeText(this, "Tag written!", Toast.LENGTH_SHORT).
show();
      } else {
        Toast.makeText(this, "Tag write failed!", Toast.LENGTH_
SHORT).show();
      }
    } else {
      Log.d("onNewIntent", "received intent isn't a NFC intent.");
    }

  } catch (Exception e) {
    Log.e("onNewIntent", e.getMessage());
  }

}
```

9. On the `onResume` method, add the following lines of code:

```java
if (NfcAdapter.ACTION_NDEF_DISCOVERED.equals(getIntent().getAc
  tion())) {
  onNewIntent(getIntent());
}
```

10. Run the application.

11. Tap a tag on your phone or simulate a tap in the NFC Simulator.

12. Exit the application and tap your phone or simulate a tap on the written tag. The application should start automatically.

How it works...

The AAR record can be placed anywhere in the NDEF message—typically in the last record—and provides a way for the Android system to identify the correct application associated with the message. We can create an application record by calling the `NdefRecord.createApplicationRecord` method and placing it in the NDEF message. When the user taps on a tag, the Android system does an initial tag scan to determine its content type and verify the presence of an AAR record. If an AAR record is present, Android tries to launch the corresponding application based on the package name present in the record. If the application is not present in the device, the Play Store is launched to download the application.

Android uses the first record present in the NDEF message to determine the content type; so, it's not the best practice to place the AAR as the first record.

Working with external types

If you are developing an application that writes a specific data object into the tag, you should use the external type records. The payload doesn't need to follow any specific structure like it does in the text records. We can also use these types to create generic records for better support in both Android and non-Android devices since these are simpler `ndef` records.

How to do it...

We are going to create an application that creates and writes an NDEF Message that contains an NFC Forum External Type-formatted `ndef` record to a tag:

Please note that this recipe requires API level 16 to run and will not work with the OpenNFC Simulator since it is sunning API level 15. It should be tested using a real device.

1. Open Eclipse and create a new Android application project named `NfcBookCh3Example5` with the package name `nfcbook.ch3.example5`.

2. Make sure the `AndroidManifest.xml` file is configured correctly (refer to the *Requesting NFC permissions* recipe in *Chapter 1, Getting Started with NFC*).

3. Set the minimum SDK version to 16:

```
<uses-sdk android:minSdkVersion="16" />
```

4. Make sure the foreground dispatch system is enabled (refer to the *Understanding the foreground dispatch system* recipe in *Chapter 2, Detecting a Tag*).

5. Open `MainActivity` located under `nfcbook.ch3.example5` and add the following class member:

```
private NfcAdapter nfcAdapter;
```

6. Instantiate the `nfcAdapter` class field in the `onCreate` method:

```
protected void onCreate(Bundle savedInstanceState) {
...
nfcAdapter = NfcAdapter.getDefaultAdapter(this);
}
```

7. Implement the `isNfcIntent`, `formatTag`, and `writeNdefMessage` methods from step 6 of the previous recipe.

8. Override the `onNewIntent` method and add the following code:

```
@Override
protected void onNewIntent(Intent intent) {

  try {

    if (isNfcIntent(intent)) {

      // additional payload
      byte[] payload = null;

      NdefRecord externalRecord = NdefRecord.
createExternal("packtpub.com", "myexternaltype", payload);

      NdefMessage ndefMessage = new NdefMessage(new NdefRecord[] {
externalRecord });

      Tag tag = intent.getParcelableExtra(NfcAdapter.EXTRA_TAG);

      if (writeNdefMessage(tag, ndefMessage)) {
        Toast.makeText(this, "Tag written!", Toast.LENGTH_SHORT).
show();
      } else {
        Toast.makeText(this, "Tag write failed!", Toast.LENGTH_
SHORT).show();
      }
```

```
    } else {
      Log.d("onNewIntent", "received intent isn't a NFC intent.");
    }

  } catch (Exception e) {
    Log.e("onNewIntent", e.getMessage());
  }

}
```

9. Run the application.
10. Tap a tag or simulate a tap in the NFC Simulator. A **Write Successful!** toast should appear.

How it works...

External type records are very similar to the URI. They are both based on the URN scheme and are basically URIs that point to a service location.

Note that the `createExternal` method receives two parameters, the domain and the type, which are then put together to create the `urn:nfc:ext:packtpub.com:myexternaltype` URI. The `urn:nfc:ext:` part of the URI is omitted according to the specification and it's not written to the tag.

Working with custom mimes

As we saw in previous recipes, an `NdefRecord` basically stores bytes so that we can virtually store anything we want. In this recipe, we will see how to create our own mime type to store a class instance.

How to do it...

We are going to create an application that creates and writes a custom, mimed `ndef` record to a tag. In this case, we will be serializing and deserializing a Java class, as described in the following steps:

1. Open Eclipse and create a new Android application project named `NfcBookCh3Example6` with the package name `com.nfcbook.ch3.example6`.

2. Make sure the `AndroidManifest.xml` file is configured correctly (refer to the *Requesting NFC permissions* recipe in *Chapter 1, Getting Started with NFC*).

3. Set the minimum SDK version to 16:

```
<uses-sdk android:minSdkVersion="16" />
```

4. Make sure the foreground dispatch system is enabled (refer to the *Understanding the foreground dispatch system* recipe in *Chapter 2, Detecting a Tag*).

5. Create a new class called `MyClass` with the following content:

```java
public class MyClass implements Serializable {

  private String myStringProp = "a string";
  private int myIntProp = 10;
  private Boolean myBoolProp = true;
  private float myFloatProp = (float) 10.5;

  public String getMyStringProp() {
    return myStringProp;
  }
  public void setMyStringProp(String myStringProp) {
    this.myStringProp = myStringProp;
  }

  public int getMyIntProp() {
    return myIntProp;
  }

  public void setMyIntProp(int myIntProp) {
    this.myIntProp = myIntProp;
  }

  public Boolean getMyBoolProp() {
    return myBoolProp;
  }

  public void setMyBoolProp(Boolean myBoolProp) {
    this.myBoolProp = myBoolProp;
  }

  public float getMyFloatProp() {
    return myFloatProp;
  }

  public void setMyFloatProp(float myFloatProp) {
    this.myFloatProp = myFloatProp;
  }
@Override
public String toString() {
    return String.format("String: %s, Int: %d, Boolean: %s, Float:
%.2f", myStringProp, myIntProp, myBoolProp, myFloatProp);
}
}
```

6. Open `MainActivity` located under `nfcbook.ch3.example6` and add the following class member:

```
private NfcAdapter nfcAdapter;
```

7. Instantiate the `nfcAdapter` class field in the `onCreate` method:

```
protected void onCreate(Bundle savedInstanceState) {
...
nfcAdapter = NfcAdapter.getDefaultAdapter(this);
}
```

8. Implement the `objectToBytes` method:

```java
byte[] objectToBytes(Object obj) {
  ByteArrayOutputStream bos = new ByteArrayOutputStream();
  ObjectOutput out = null;

  try {
    out = new ObjectOutputStream(bos);
    out.writeObject(obj);
    out.close();
    bos.close();

  } catch (Exception e) {
    Log.e("objectToBytes", e.getMessage());
  }

  return bos.toByteArray();
}
```

9. Implement the `bytesToObject` method:

```java
Object bytesToObject(byte[] bytes) {
  Object o = null;
  ByteArrayInputStream bis = new ByteArrayInputStream(bytes);
  ObjectInput in = null;

  try {
    in = new ObjectInputStream(bis);

    o = in.readObject();

    bis.close();
  } catch (Exception e) {
    Log.e("bytesToObject", e.getMessage());
  }
  return o;
}
```

10. Implement the `isNfcIntent`, `formatTag`, and `writeNdefMessage` methods from step 7 of the previous recipe.

11. Override the `onNewIntent` method and add the following code:

```
@Override
protected void onNewIntent(Intent intent) {

  try {
    if (isNfcIntent(intent)) {

        NdefRecord mimeRecord = NdefRecord.createMime("application/
vnd." + this.getPackageName() + ".MyClass", objectToBytes(new
MyClass()));

        NdefMessage ndefMessage = new NdefMessage(new NdefRecord[] {
mimeRecord });

        Tag tag = intent.getParcelableExtra(NfcAdapter.EXTRA_TAG);
        if (writeNdefMessage(tag, ndefMessage)) {
          Toast.makeText(this, "Tag written!", Toast.LENGTH_SHORT).
show();
        } else {
          Toast.makeText(this, "Tag write failed!", Toast.LENGTH_
SHORT).show();
        }
    }

  } catch (Exception e) {
    Log.e("onNewIntent", e.getMessage());
  }

}
```

12. Run the application.

13. Tap a tag on your phone or simulate a tap in the NFC Simulator. A **Write Successful!** toast should appear.

How it works...

Custom mime records open up the possibility to create records whose content is recognized worldwide, such as images, HTML pages, and document files (if the tag has enough memory). These types of records should be preferred while we are working with already known mime types, but we can also create our own custom mime (like we did in this recipe). This can be useful to allow different developers' applications to exchange data in a previously defined structure; otherwise, we can use the NFC Forum External Types record.

We can create a custom mime record by calling the `NdefRecord.createMime` method and passing our mime name as the first parameter and a byte array representation of our data. This byte array can then be accessed in the read tag operation by calling the `getPayload` method of the record.

We can filter tags by our custom mime name; refer to the *Filtering tags by their content type* recipe in *Chapter 2, Detecting a Tag*.

We can use the `createMime` method not only to create our custom mimes but also to create well-known mime types such as images/PNG, applications/JSON, and so on.

4
Writing Tag Content – Real-life Examples

In this chapter, we will cover the following topics:

- Making a phone call with one tap – Part 1
- Sending a predefined SMS – Part 1
- Visiting our website
- Leaving a (small) note – Part 1

Introduction

In this chapter, we will create some applications that are actually used in real-life scenarios. We can use them on a daily basis to simplify repetitive tasks.

For simplicity purposes, the methods related to tags and NDEF Records handling, which we used in *Chapter 2, Detecting a Tag*, and *Chapter 3, Writing Tag Content*, were placed in the `NfcHelper` class. This class will to be used in every Android-related recipe and is described in the following code:

```java
public class NfcHelper {
  public NfcHelper(Activity activity){...}

  public boolean isNfcEnabledDevice(){...}

  public boolean isNfcIntent(Intent intent){...}

  public Tag getTagFromIntent(Intent intent){...}
```

```java
public void enableForegroundDispatch(){...}

public void disableForegroundDispatch(){...}

public boolean writeNdefMessage(Intent intent, NdefMessage
ndefMessage){...}

public boolean writeNdefMessage(Tag tag, NdefMessage ndefMessage)
{...}

private boolean formatTag(Tag tag, NdefMessage ndefMessage){...}

public NdefRecord createUriRecord(String uri){...}

public NdefRecord createTextRecord(String content){...}

public NdefMessage createUrlNdefMessage(String uri){...}

public NdefMessage createTextNdefMessage(String text) {...}
}
```

The full implementation of the `NfcHelper` class can be found in the downloadable content.

Making a phone call with one tap – Part 1

A lot of people make several phone calls in a day to the same people in repetitive ways Getting in touch with a boyfriend/girlfriend, calling your parents' home, or even when your boss always keeps calling you for meetings at work, are some examples of where you could use NFC to make this communication easier. Imagine that your office has NFC sticker tags with images of people on your contact list. You could call any person on that list when you tap the tag, thus avoiding the need to open the contact list, search for that person, and then initiate the call.

Getting ready

- Make sure you have a working Android development environment. If you don't, ADT Bundle is a good kit to start with. You can download it from `http://developer.android.com/sdk/index.html`.

- Make sure you have an NFC-enabled Android device or a virtual test environment—refer to the *Testing your app all together* recipe in *Chapter 1, Getting Started with NFC*.

- It will be assumed that Eclipse is the development IDE and also that you are familiar with creating URI-formatted NDEF Records—refer to the *Writing a URI-formatted record* recipe in *Chapter 3, Writing Tag Content*.

How to do it...

In the first part of the development of this application, we will allow the user to write a phone number in the application and save it in a tag. The user can also go to the contact list and share a contact with the application, avoiding the need to write the number themselves. This can be done with the following steps:

1. Open Eclipse and create a new Android application project named `NfcBookCh4PhoneCall` and a package named `nfcbook.ch4phonecall`.

2. Make sure the `AndroidManifest.xml` file is configured correctly—refer to the *Requesting NFC permissions* recipe in *Chapter 1, Getting Started with NFC*—and add the following lines of code inside the `<activity>` element:

```xml
<intent-filter>
  <action android:name="android.intent.action.SEND" />
  <category android:name="android.intent.category.DEFAULT"
    />
  <data android:mimeType="text/x-vcard" />
</intent-filter>
```

Our activity will now be able to receive intents with the `text/x-vcard` mime type, which means that a user can share a contact with our application. Then, we can read the contact's phone number and place it in `EditText`.

3. Add the following content to the `strings.xml` file located at `/res/values`:

```xml
<string name="label_phone_number">Phone Number</string>
<string name="button_write_tag">Write Tag</string>
<string name="label_no_nfc">NFC is not available on this device</
string>
<string name="toast_write_successful">Write Successful!</string>
<string name="toast_write_fail">Write Failed!</string>
<string name="toast_phone_number_missing ">Phone Number missing!</
string>
<string name="dialog_tap_on_tag">Tap on a Tag!</string>
<string name="label_smile_sad">:(</string>
```

The previous strings are used both in layouts and in code files, allowing us to not hard code the user message and the layout information.

4. Replace the content of the `activity_main.xml` file located at `/res/layout` with the following code:

```xml
<RelativeLayout xmlns:android="http://schemas.android.com/apk/res/
android"
    xmlns:tools="http://schemas.android.com/tools"
    android:layout_width="match_parent"
```

```xml
    android:layout_height="match_parent"
    android:paddingBottom="@dimen/activity_vertical_margin"
    android:paddingLeft="@dimen/activity_horizontal_margin"
    android:paddingRight="@dimen/activity_horizontal_margin"
    android:paddingTop="@dimen/activity_vertical_margin"
    tools:context=".MainActivity" >

    <TextView
        android:id="@+id/lblPhoneNumber"
        android:layout_width="wrap_content"
        android:layout_height="wrap_content"
        android:layout_alignParentLeft="true"
        android:layout_alignParentRight="true"
        android:layout_alignParentTop="true"
        android:text="@string/label_phone_number" />

    <EditText
        android:id="@+id/txtPhoneNumber"
        android:layout_width="wrap_content"
        android:layout_height="wrap_content"
        android:layout_alignParentLeft="true"
        android:layout_alignRight="@+id/lblPhoneNumber"
        android:layout_below="@+id/lblPhoneNumber"
        android:ems="10"
        android:layout_marginTop="10dp"
        android:inputType="phone" >

        <requestFocus />
    </EditText>

    <Button
        android:id="@+id/btWriteTag"
        style="?android:attr/buttonStyleSmall"
        android:layout_width="wrap_content"
        android:layout_height="wrap_content"
        android:layout_alignParentBottom="true"
        android:layout_alignParentLeft="true"
        android:layout_alignParentRight="true"
        android:text="@string/button_write_tag"
        android:onClick="onBtWriteTagClick" />

</RelativeLayout>
```

This creates a layout that is identical to the following screenshot:

The previous layout is the main application layout and allows the user to fill in the phone number that will be written in the tag when they press the **Write Tag** button.

5. Add a layout file to the project named `activity_main_no_nfc.xml` and replace the content with the following code:

```xml
<LinearLayout xmlns:android="http://schemas.android.com/apk/res/
android"
    android:layout_width="fill_parent"
    android:layout_height="fill_parent"
    android:orientation="vertical" >

    <TextView
        android:layout_width="match_parent"
        android:layout_height="0dip"
        android:layout_weight="1"
        android:gravity="center_horizontal|center_vertical"
        android:text="@string/label_smile_sad"
        android:textSize="100sp" />

    <TextView
        android:layout_width="match_parent"
        android:layout_height="40dp"
```

```
        android:gravity="center_horizontal|center_vertical"
        android:text="@string/label_no_nfc"
        android:textAppearance="?android:attr/
textAppearanceMedium" />

</LinearLayout>
```

This creates a layout that is identical to the following screenshot:

The previous layout will be shown to the user if the NFC doesn't have a compatible device.

6. Include the `NfcHelper` class in the project under the same package as `MainActivity`.

7. Open `MainActivity` located under `nfcbook.ch4phonecall` and add the following class members before the `onCreate` method:

```
NfcHelper nfcHelper;
TextView txtPhoneNumber;

Boolean isWritingTag = false;
ProgressDialog writingProgressDialog;
```

8. Replace the `onCreate` method with the following code:

```
@Override
protected void onCreate(Bundle savedInstanceState) {
```

```java
    super.onCreate(savedInstanceState);

    nfcHelper = new NfcHelper(this);

    if (!nfcHelper.isNfcEnabledDevice()) {
      setContentView(R.layout.activity_main_no_nfc);
      return;
    }
    setContentView(R.layout.activity_main);

    txtPhoneNumber = (TextView) findViewById(R.id.txtPhoneNumber);

    handleIntent(getIntent());
  }
```

This is where we test whether the device is compatible and choose which layout to display.

9. Override the `onResume` method and add the following code:

```java
@Override
protected void onResume() {
  super.onResume();

  if (nfcHelper.isNfcEnabledDevice()) {
    nfcHelper.enableForegroundDispatch();
  }
}
```

10. Override the `onPause` method and add the following code:

```java
@Override
protected void onPause() {
  super.onPause();

  if (nfcHelper.isNfcEnabledDevice()) {
    nfcHelper.disableForegroundDispatch();
  }
}
```

This allows us to enable and disable the foreground dispatch system.

11. Override the `onNewIntent` method and add the following code:

```java
@Override
protected void onNewIntent(Intent intent) {
```

```
    if (nfcHelper.isNfcIntent(intent)) {

      if (isWritingTag) {

        NdefMessage ndefMsg = nfcHelper.createUrlNdefMessage("tel:"
+ txtPhoneNumber.getText().toString());

          if (nfcHelper.writeNdefMessage(intent, ndefMsg)) {
            Toast.makeText(this, R.string.toast_write_successful,
Toast.LENGTH_LONG).show();
          } else {
            Toast.makeText(this, R.string.toast_write_fail, Toast.
LENGTH_LONG).show();
          }

        isWritingTag = false;
        writingProgressDialog.dismiss();

      } else {

        // Check Chapter 5 to know how to get tag content

      }
    } else {
      handleIntent(intent);
    }
}
```

This is where the tag gets written when the user taps a tag after pressing the **Write Tag** button.

12. Implement the `handleIntent` method as shown in the following code:

```
public void handleIntent(Intent intent) {

    String action = intent.getAction();
    String type = intent.getType();

    if (Intent.ACTION_SEND.equals(action) && type != null) {
      if ("text/x-vcard".equals(type)) {

        Uri uri = (Uri) intent.getExtras().get(Intent.EXTRA_STREAM);
        readVCard(uri);
      }
    }
}
```

The `handleIntent` method is responsible for verifying whether the incoming intent contains a vCard and calling the `readVCard` method.

13. Implement the `readVCard` method with the following code:

```java
private void readVCard(Uri uri) {

  try {

      //opens v-card file and load its content to a string
      ContentResolver cr = getContentResolver();
      InputStream inputStream = cr.openInputStream(uri);

      BufferedReader reader = new BufferedReader(new InputStreamRead
er(inputStream));

      StringBuilder fileContent = new StringBuilder();
      String line;
      while ((line = reader.readLine()) != null) {
        fileContent.append(line);
      }

      String data = fileContent.toString();

      //tries to find a phone number
      Pattern pattern = Pattern.compile("\\d{3}-\\d{3}-\\d{3}");
      Matcher matcher = pattern.matcher(data);

      if (matcher.find()) {
        txtPhoneNumber.setText(matcher.group(0));
      }

  } catch (Exception e) {
    Log.e("readVCard", "error reading vcard", e);
  }
}
```

In this method we get the `vCard` file, where we can read its content and try to extract a phone number from it.

14. Implement the `onBtWriteTagClick` method with the following code:

```java
public void onBtWriteTagClick(View view) {
   String phoneNumber = txtPhoneNumber.getText().toString();

   if (phoneNumber.isEmpty()) {

      Toast.makeText(this, R.string.toast_phone_number_missing,
   Toast.LENGTH_LONG).show();

      return;
   }

   showWaitDialog();
}
```

15. Implement the `showWaitDialog` method with the following code:

```java
private void showWaitDialog() {

   writingProgressDialog = ProgressDialog.show(this, "",
   getString(R.string.dialog_tap_on_tag), false, true, new
   OnCancelListener() {

      @Override
      public void onCancel(DialogInterface arg0) {
         isWritingTag = false;
      }
   });

   isWritingTag = true;

}
```

16. Run the application, type in a phone number, or open the contact list, choose a contact, and share it to the `NfcBookCh4PhoneCall` application. Press the **Write Tag** button.

17. Tap your phone on a tag or simulate a tap in NFC Simulator. A **Write Successful!** toast should appear.

How it works...

When the application starts, we validate whether the device is an NFC-enabled device and display a different layout based on this validation. If it fails, we display a "sad face" layout—`activity_main_no_nfc.xml`—and avoid unhandled exceptions this way. Otherwise, the `activity_main.xml` layout is displayed, and it allows the user to type the number to write in the tag. This activity can also receive a vCard from other applications that use the share functionality, such as the native contact application, and extract the phone number from it. This functionality is achieved by adding a second intent filter to `MainActivity` in the manifest file for the `text/x-vcard` type and calling the `handleIntent` method.

Because writing on a tag depends on a user's action, we display a simple progress bar after the **Write Tag** button is pressed to let the user know that we are waiting for them to tap on a tag. When that happens, the `onNewIntent` method gets called by the foreground dispatch system, and we write a URI-formatted record that contains a URI based on a standard schema to make phone calls—`tel:[PHONE-NUMBER]`. This schema is used in web applications as well and is recognized by the Android system.

Use standards whenever possible! This way we can create more compatible applications and our work is facilitated. In this case, Android recognizes those URI schemas, and we will not need to work much to obtain and handle the saved URIs in Part 2 of this recipe.

Sending a predefined SMS – Part 1

In this recipe, we will see how to store an SMS and the recipient in a tag, which we will retrieve and handle later. You can find the Part 2 of this recipe in *Chapter 6, Reading Tag Content – Real-life Examples*.

How to do it...

In the first part of the development of this application, we will allow the user to write a phone number and the SMS in the application and save them in a tag. Users can also go to the contact list and share a contact with the application, avoiding the need to write the number on their own. This can be done with the following steps:

1. Open Eclipse and create a new Android application project named `NfcBookCh4SMS` and a package named `nfcbook.ch4sms`.

2. Make sure the `AndroidManifest.xml` file is configured correctly —refer to the *Requesting NFC permissions* recipe in *Chapter 1, Getting Started with NFC*.

3. Add the following lines of code inside the `<activity>` element:

```xml
<intent-filter>
  <action android:name="android.intent.action.SEND" />
  <category android:name="android.intent.category.DEFAULT" />
  <data android:mimeType="text/x-vcard" />
</intent-filter>
```

4. Add the following content to the `strings.xml` file located at `/res/values`:

```xml
<string name="label_phone_number">Phone Number</string>
<string name="button_write_tag">Write Tag</string>
<string name="toast_write_successful">Write Successful!</string>
<string name="toast_write_fail">Write Failed!</string>
<string name="label_no_nfc">NFC is not available on this device</string>
<string name="toast_phone_number_missing ">Phone Number missing!</string>
<string name="dialog_tap_on_tag">Tap on a Tag!</string>
<string name="label_sms_body">Sms Body</string>
<string name="label_smile_sad">:(</string>
```

5. Replace the content of the `activity_main.xml` file located at `/res/layout` with the following code:

```xml
<RelativeLayout xmlns:android="http://schemas.android.com/apk/res/android"
    xmlns:tools="http://schemas.android.com/tools"
    android:layout_width="match_parent"
    android:layout_height="match_parent"
    android:paddingBottom="@dimen/activity_vertical_margin"
    android:paddingLeft="@dimen/activity_horizontal_margin"
    android:paddingRight="@dimen/activity_horizontal_margin"
    android:paddingTop="@dimen/activity_vertical_margin"
    tools:context=".MainActivity" >

    <EditText
        android:id="@+id/txtSmsBody"
        android:layout_width="wrap_content"
        android:layout_height="wrap_content"
        android:layout_above="@+id/btWriteTag"
        android:layout_alignParentLeft="true"
        android:layout_alignParentRight="true"
        android:layout_below="@+id/lblSmsBody"
        android:layout_marginTop="10dp"
        android:ems="10"
        android:inputType="textMultiLine" >
```

```xml
        <requestFocus />
    </EditText>

    <Button
        android:id="@+id/btWriteTag"
        style="?android:attr/buttonStyleSmall"
        android:layout_width="wrap_content"
        android:layout_height="wrap_content"
        android:layout_alignParentBottom="true"
        android:layout_alignParentLeft="true"
        android:layout_alignParentRight="true"
        android:onClick="onBtWriteTagClick"
        android:text="@string/button_write_tag" />

    <TextView
        android:id="@+id/lblPhoneNumber"
        android:layout_width="wrap_content"
        android:layout_height="wrap_content"
        android:layout_alignParentLeft="true"
        android:layout_alignParentRight="true"
        android:layout_alignParentTop="true"
        android:text="@string/label_phone_number" />

    <EditText
        android:id="@+id/txtPhoneNumber"
        android:layout_width="wrap_content"
        android:layout_height="wrap_content"
        android:layout_alignParentLeft="true"
        android:layout_alignParentRight="true"
        android:layout_below="@+id/lblPhoneNumber"
        android:ems="10"
        android:inputType="phone" />

    <TextView
        android:id="@+id/lblSmsBody"
        android:layout_width="wrap_content"
        android:layout_height="wrap_content"
        android:layout_alignLeft="@+id/txtPhoneNumber"
        android:layout_alignParentRight="true"
        android:layout_below="@+id/txtPhoneNumber"
        android:layout_marginTop="20dp"
        android:text="@string/label_sms_body" />
</RelativeLayout>
```

The previous code creates a layout that is identical to the following screenshot:

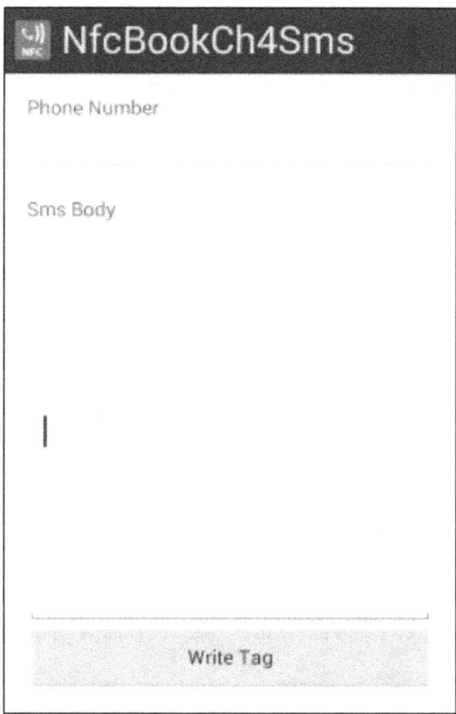

6. Add a layout file to the project named `activity_main_no_nfc.xml` and replace the content with the following code:

```xml
<LinearLayout xmlns:android="http://schemas.android.com/apk/res/
android"
    android:layout_width="fill_parent"
    android:layout_height="fill_parent"
    android:orientation="vertical" >

    <TextView
        android:layout_width="match_parent"
        android:layout_height="0dip"
        android:layout_weight="1"
        android:gravity="center_horizontal|center_vertical"
        android:text="@string/label_smile_sad"
        android:textSize="100sp" />
```

```
<TextView
    android:layout_width="match_parent"
    android:layout_height="40dp"
    android:gravity="center_horizontal|center_vertical"
    android:text="@string/label_no_nfc"
    android:textAppearance="?android:attr/
textAppearanceMedium" />

</LinearLayout>
```

This creates a layout that is identical to the following screenshot:

7. Include the `NfcHelper` class in the project under the same package as `MainActivity`.

8. Open `MainActivity` located under `nfcbook.ch4sms` and add the following class members before the `onCreate` method:

```
NfcHelper nfcHelper;
TextView txtPhoneNumber;
TextView txtSmsBody;
Boolean isWritingTag = false;
ProgressDialog writingProgressDialog;
```

9. Override the `onCreate` method and add the following code:

```java
@Override
protected void onCreate(Bundle savedInstanceState) {
  super.onCreate(savedInstanceState);

  nfcHelper = new NfcHelper(this);

  if (!nfcHelper.isNfcEnabledDevice()) {
    setContentView(R.layout.activity_main_no_nfc);
    return;
  }

  setContentView(R.layout.activity_main);

  txtPhoneNumber = (TextView) findViewById(R.id.txtPhoneNumber);
  txtSmsBody = (TextView) findViewById(R.id.txtSmsBody);

  handleIntent(getIntent());
}
```

10. Override the `onResume` method and add the following code:

```java
@Override
protected void onResume() {
  super.onResume();

  if (nfcHelper.isNfcEnabledDevice()) {
    nfcHelper.enableForegroundDispatch();
  }
}
```

11. Override the `onPause` method and add the following code:

```java
@Override
protected void onPause() {
  super.onPause();

  if (nfcHelper.isNfcEnabledDevice()) {
    nfcHelper.disableForegroundDispatch();
  }
}
```

12. Override the `onNewIntent` method and add the following code:

```java
@Override
protected void onNewIntent(Intent intent) {

  if (nfcHelper.isNfcIntent(intent)) {
    if (isWritingTag) {

      String smsUri = String.format("sms:%s?body=%s",
txtPhoneNumber.getText().toString(), URLEncoder.encode(txtSmsBody.
getText().toString()));

      NdefMessage ndefMsg = nfcHelper.
createUrlNdefMessage(smsUri);

      if (nfcHelper.writeNdefMessage(intent, ndefMsg)) {

        Toast.makeText(this, R.string.toast_write_successful,
Toast.LENGTH_LONG).show();
      } else {

        Toast.makeText(this, R.string.toast_write_fail, Toast.
LENGTH_LONG).show();

      }

      isWritingTag = false;
      writingProgressDialog.dismiss();

    } else {

      // Check Chapter 5 to know how to get tag content

    }
  }
}
```

13. Implement the `handleIntent` method with the following code:

```java
public void handleIntent(Intent intent) {

  String action = intent.getAction();
  String type = intent.getType();
```

```java
        if (Intent.ACTION_SEND.equals(action) && type != null) {
          if ("text/x-vcard".equals(type)) {

            Uri uri = (Uri) intent.getExtras().get(Intent.EXTRA_STREAM);
            readVCard(uri);

          }
        }
      }
```

14. Implement the `readVCard` method:

```java
    private void readVCard(Uri uri) {

      try {

        // open's v-card file and load its content to a string
        ContentResolver cr = getContentResolver();
        InputStream inputStream = cr.openInputStream(uri);

        BufferedReader reader = new BufferedReader(new InputStreamRead
    er(inputStream));

        StringBuilder fileContent = new StringBuilder();
        String line;
        while ((line = reader.readLine()) != null) {
          fileContent.append(line);
        }

        String data = fileContent.toString();

        // tries to find a phone number
        Pattern pattern = Pattern.compile("\\d{3}-\\d{3}-\\d{3}");
        Matcher matcher = pattern.matcher(data);

        if (matcher.find()) {
          txtPhoneNumber.setText(matcher.group(0));
        }

      } catch (Exception e) {
        Log.e("readVCard", "error reading vcard", e);
      }
    }
```

15. Implement the `onBtWriteTagClick` method with the following code:

```java
public void onBtWriteTagClick(View view) {
  String phoneNumber = txtPhoneNumber.getText().toString();

  if (phoneNumber.isEmpty()) {

    Toast.makeText(this, R.string.toast_phone_number_missing,
  Toast.LENGTH_LONG).show();

    return;
  }

  showWaitDialog();
}
```

16. Implement the `showWaitDialog` method with the following code:

```java
private void showWaitDialog() {

  writingProgressDialog = ProgressDialog.show(this, "",
  getString(R.string.dialog_tap_on_tag), false, true, new
  OnCancelListener() {

    @Override
    public void onCancel(DialogInterface arg0) {
      isWritingTag = false;
    }
  });

  isWritingTag = true;

}
```

17. Run the application, type in a phone number, or open the contact list, choose a contact, and share it to the `NfcBookCh4SMS` application. Type an SMS and press the **Write Tag** button.

18. Tap your phone on a tag or simulate a tap in NFC Simulator. A **Write Successful!** toast should appear.

How it works...

Because writing on a tag depends on a user's action, we display a simple progress bar after the **Write Tag** button is pressed to let the user know that we are waiting for them to tap on a tag. When that happens, the `onNewIntent` method gets called by the foreground dispatch system, and we write a URI-formatted record that contains URIs based on a standard schema to send an SMS—`sms:[PHONE-NUMBER]` and `sms:[PHONE-NUMBER]?body=[MESSAGE]`. This schema is used in web applications as well and is recognized by the Android system (the body parameter is only recognized in Android Version 4 onwards).

Visiting our website

NFC tags come in a variety of sizes and formats. One of these formats is the business card. Imagine how cool it would be for people to open your company website with just a tap! Besides having a very unique business card, you will get people directed to the website very quickly. Through this application, we will be able to store a website's URL in a tag easily.

How to do it...

In this first part of the development of this application, we will allow the user to write a URL in the application and save it in a tag. User can also go to the web browser and share a link to the application, avoiding the need to write it themselves. This can be done with the following steps:

1. Open Eclipse and create a new Android application project named `NfcBookCh4WebLink` and a package named `nfcbook.ch4weblink`.

2. Make sure the `AndroidManifest.xml` file is configured correctly —refer to the *Requesting NFC permissions* recipe in *Chapter 1, Getting Started with NFC*.

3. Add the following lines of code inside the `<activity>` element:

```xml
<intent-filter>
    <action android:name="android.intent.action.SEND" />
    <category android:name="android.intent.category.DEFAULT" />
    <data android:mimeType="text/plain" />
</intent-filter>
```

4. Add the following content to the `strings.xml` file located at `/res/values`:

```xml
<string name="button_write_tag">Write Tag</string>
<string name="label_no_nfc">NFC is not available on this device</string>
<string name="toast_write_successful">Write Successful!</string>
<string name="toast_write_fail">Write Failed!</string>
```

```xml
<string name="dialog_tap_on_tag">Tap on a Tag!</string>
<string name="label_smile_sad">:(</string>
<string name="label_web_link">Web link</string>
<string name="toast_invalid_url">Invalid url!</string>
```

5. Replace the content of the `activity_main.xml` file located at `/res/layout` with the following code:

```xml
<RelativeLayout xmlns:android="http://schemas.android.com/apk/res/
android"
    xmlns:tools="http://schemas.android.com/tools"
    android:layout_width="match_parent"
    android:layout_height="match_parent"
    android:paddingBottom="@dimen/activity_vertical_margin"
    android:paddingLeft="@dimen/activity_horizontal_margin"
    android:paddingRight="@dimen/activity_horizontal_margin"
    android:paddingTop="@dimen/activity_vertical_margin"
    tools:context=".MainActivity" >

    <EditText
        android:id="@+id/txtWebLink"
        android:layout_width="wrap_content"
        android:layout_height="wrap_content"
        android:layout_above="@+id/btWriteTag"
        android:layout_alignParentLeft="true"
        android:layout_alignParentRight="true"
        android:layout_below="@+id/lblWebLink"
        android:layout_marginTop="10dp"
        android:ems="10"
        android:inputType="textMultiLine" >

        <requestFocus />
    </EditText>

    <Button
        android:id="@+id/btWriteTag"
        style="?android:attr/buttonStyleSmall"
        android:layout_width="wrap_content"
        android:layout_height="wrap_content"
        android:layout_alignParentBottom="true"
        android:layout_alignParentLeft="true"
        android:layout_alignParentRight="true"
        android:onClick="onBtWriteTagClick"
        android:text="@string/button_write_tag" />
```

```
<TextView
    android:id="@+id/lblWebLink"
    android:layout_width="wrap_content"
    android:layout_height="wrap_content"
    android:layout_alignParentLeft="true"
    android:layout_alignParentRight="true"
    android:layout_alignParentTop="true"
    android:text="@string/label_web_link" />

</RelativeLayout>
```

The previous code creates a layout that is identical to the following screenshot:

6. Add a layout file to the project named `activity_main_no_nfc.xml` and replace the content with the following code:

```
<LinearLayout xmlns:android="http://schemas.android.com/apk/res/
android"
    android:layout_width="fill_parent"
    android:layout_height="fill_parent"
    android:orientation="vertical" >

    <TextView
        android:layout_width="match_parent"
        android:layout_height="0dip"
```

```
        android:layout_weight="1"
        android:gravity="center_horizontal|center_vertical"
        android:text="@string/label_smile_sad"
        android:textSize="100sp" />

    <TextView
        android:layout_width="match_parent"
        android:layout_height="40dp"
        android:gravity="center_horizontal|center_vertical"
        android:text="@string/label_no_nfc"
        android:textAppearance="?android:attr/
textAppearanceMedium" />

</LinearLayout>
```

This should create a layout that is identical to the following screenshot:

7. Include the `NfcHelper` class in the project under the same package as `MainActivity`.

8. Open `MainActivity` located under `nfcbook.ch4weblink` and add the following class members before the `onCreate` method:

```
NfcHelper nfcHelper;
TextView txtWebLink;

Boolean isWritingTag = false;
ProgressDialog writingProgressDialog;
```

9. Override the `onCreate` method and add the following code:

```
@Override
protected void onCreate(Bundle savedInstanceState) {
  super.onCreate(savedInstanceState);

  nfcHelper = new NfcHelper(this);

  if (!nfcHelper.isNfcEnabledDevice()) {
    setContentView(R.layout.activity_main_no_nfc);
    return;
  }

  setContentView(R.layout.activity_main);

  txtWebLink = (TextView) findViewById(R.id.txtWebLink);

  handleIntent(getIntent());
}
```

10. Override the `onResume` method and add the following code:

```
@Override
protected void onResume() {
  super.onResume();

  if (nfcHelper.isNfcEnabledDevice()) {
    nfcHelper.enableForegroundDispatch();
  }
}
```

11. Override the `onPause` method and add the following code:

```
@Override
protected void onPause() {
  super.onPause();

  if (nfcHelper.isNfcEnabledDevice()) {
```

```java
        nfcHelper.disableForegroundDispatch();
    }
}
```

12. Override the `onNewIntent` method and add the following code:

```java
@Override
protected void onNewIntent(Intent intent) {

    if (nfcHelper.isNfcIntent(intent)) {
        if (isWritingTag) {

            String url = txtWebLink.getText().toString();

            NdefMessage ndefMsg = nfcHelper.createUrlNdefMessage(url);

            if (nfcHelper.writeNdefMessage(intent, ndefMsg)) {
                Toast.makeText(this, R.string.toast_write_successful,
Toast.LENGTH_LONG).show();
            } else {
                Toast.makeText(this, R.string.toast_write_fail, Toast.
LENGTH_LONG).show();
            }

            isWritingTag = false;
            writingProgressDialog.dismiss();

        } else {

            // Check Chapter 5 to know how to get tag content

        }
    }
}
```

13. Implement the `handleIntent` method with the following code:

```java
public void handleIntent(Intent intent) {

    String action = intent.getAction();
    String type = intent.getType();

    if (Intent.ACTION_SEND.equals(action) && type != null) {
        if ("text/plain".equals(type)) {
```

```
        String sharedText = intent.getStringExtra(Intent.EXTRA_
TEXT);
        if (sharedText != null) {
        txtWebLink.setText(sharedText);
        }


        }
    }
}
```

14. Implement the `onBtWriteTagClick` method with the following code:

```
public void onBtWriteTagClick(View view) {
  String url = txtWebLink.getText().toString();

  if (url.isEmpty() || !URLUtil.isValidUrl(url)) {
    Toast.makeText(this, R.string.toast_invalid_url, Toast.LENGTH_
LONG).show();

    return;
  }

  showWaitDialog();
}
```

15. Implement the `showWaitDialog` method with the following code:

```
private void showWaitDialog() {

    writingProgressDialog = ProgressDialog.show(this, "",
getString(R.string.dialog_tap_on_tag), false, true, new
OnCancelListener() {

      @Override
      public void onCancel(DialogInterface arg0) {
        isWritingTag = false;
      }
    });

    isWritingTag = true;

}
```

16. Run the application, type in a website's URL, or open your browser, then go to a website and share it to the `NfcBookCh4WebLink` application. Press the **Write Tag** button.

17. Tap your phone on a tag or simulate a tap in NFC Simulator. A **Write Successful!** toast should appear.

How it works...

Much like in the previous recipes, we will first validate whether the device has NFC and whether it displays a different layout based on the validations, avoiding unhandled exceptions. The `onNewIntent` method is the one responsible for writing the desired URL into the tag that has been previously validated in the `onBtWriteTagClick` method.

For a better user experience, we allow our activity to receive simple text content so that the user can share a URL from the browser to our application, saving him some efforts.

Leaving a (small) note – Part 1

In this recipe, we will see how to store a text block in a tag, which we will retrieve and handle later—Part 2 of this recipe in *Chapter 6, Reading Tag Content – Real-life Examples*.

How to do it...

In the first part of the development of this application, we are going to allow the user to write some text in the application and save it in a tag. The user can also go to any other application that supports content sharing and share some text with the application, avoiding the need to write the note on his/her own.

1. Open Eclipse and create a new Android application project named `NfcBookCh4Note` and a package named `nfcbook.ch4note`.

2. Make sure the `AndroidManifest.xml` file is configured correctly —refer to the *Requesting NFC permissions* recipe in *Chapter 1, Getting Started with NFC*.

3. Add the following lines of code inside the `<activity>` element:

```xml
<intent-filter>
  <action android:name="android.intent.action.SEND" />
  <category android:name="android.intent.category.DEFAULT" />
  <data android:mimeType="text/plain" />
</intent-filter>
```

4. Add the following content to the `strings.xml` file located at `/res/values`:

```xml
<string name="button_write_tag">Write Tag</string>
<string name="label_no_nfc">NFC is not available on this device</string>
<string name="toast_write_successful">Write Successful!</string>
<string name="toast_write_fail">Write Failed!</string>
<string name="dialog_tap_on_tag">Tap on a Tag!</string>
<string name="label_smile_sad">:(</string>
<string name="toast_invalid_note">Invalid note!</string>
<string name="label_note">Note</string>
```

5. Replace the content of the `activity_main.xml` file located at `/res/layout` with the following code:

```xml
<RelativeLayout xmlns:android="http://schemas.android.com/apk/res/
android"
    xmlns:tools="http://schemas.android.com/tools"
    android:layout_width="match_parent"
    android:layout_height="match_parent"
    android:paddingBottom="@dimen/activity_vertical_margin"
    android:paddingLeft="@dimen/activity_horizontal_margin"
    android:paddingRight="@dimen/activity_horizontal_margin"
    android:paddingTop="@dimen/activity_vertical_margin"
    tools:context=".MainActivity" >

    <EditText
        android:id="@+id/txtNote"
        android:layout_width="wrap_content"
        android:layout_height="wrap_content"
        android:layout_above="@+id/btWriteTag"
        android:layout_alignParentLeft="true"
        android:layout_alignParentRight="true"
        android:layout_below="@+id/lblNote"
        android:layout_marginTop="10dp"
        android:ems="10"
        android:inputType="textMultiLine" >

        <requestFocus />
    </EditText>

    <Button
        android:id="@+id/btWriteTag"
        style="?android:attr/buttonStyleSmall"
        android:layout_width="wrap_content"
        android:layout_height="wrap_content"
        android:layout_alignParentBottom="true"
        android:layout_alignParentLeft="true"
        android:layout_alignParentRight="true"
        android:onClick="onBtWriteTagClick"
        android:text="@string/button_write_tag" />

    <TextView
        android:id="@+id/lblNote"
        android:layout_width="wrap_content"
        android:layout_height="wrap_content"
```

```
        android:layout_alignParentLeft="true"
        android:layout_alignParentRight="true"
        android:layout_alignParentTop="true"
        android:text="@string/label_note" />

</RelativeLayout>
```

The previous code should create a layout that is identical to the following screenshot:

6. Add a layout file to the project named `activity_main_no_nfc.xml` and replace the content with the following code:

```
<LinearLayout xmlns:android="http://schemas.android.com/apk/res/
android"
    android:layout_width="fill_parent"
    android:layout_height="fill_parent"
    android:orientation="vertical" >

    <TextView
        android:layout_width="match_parent"
        android:layout_height="0dip"
```

```
            android:layout_weight="1"
            android:gravity="center_horizontal|center_vertical"
            android:text="@string/label_smile_sad"
            android:textSize="100sp" />

    <TextView
            android:layout_width="match_parent"
            android:layout_height="40dp"
            android:gravity="center_horizontal|center_vertical"
            android:text="@string/label_no_nfc"
            android:textAppearance="?android:attr/
textAppearanceMedium" />

</LinearLayout>
```

This creates a layout that is identical to the following screenshot:

7. Include the `NfcHelper` class in the project under the same package as `MainActivity`.

8. Open `MainActivity` located under `com.nfcbook.ch4note`.

9. Add the following class properties before the `onCreate` method:

```
NfcHelper nfcHelper;
TextView txtNote;
```

```java
Boolean isWritingTag = false;
ProgressDialog writingProgressDialog;
```

10. Override the `onCreate` method and add the following code:

```java
@Override
protected void onCreate(Bundle savedInstanceState) {
  super.onCreate(savedInstanceState);

  nfcHelper = new NfcHelper(this);

  if (!nfcHelper.isNfcEnabledDevice()) {
    setContentView(R.layout.activity_main_no_nfc);
    return;
  }

  setContentView(R.layout.activity_main);

  txtNote = (TextView) findViewById(R.id.txtNote);

  handleIntent(getIntent());
}
```

11. Override the `onResume` method and add the following code:

```java
@Override
protected void onResume() {
  super.onResume();

  if (nfcHelper.isNfcEnabledDevice()) {
    nfcHelper.enableForegroundDispatch();
  }
}
```

12. Override the `onPause` method and add the following code:

```java
@Override
protected void onPause() {
  super.onPause();
  if (nfcHelper.isNfcEnabledDevice()) {
    nfcHelper.disableForegroundDispatch();
  }
}
```

13. Override the `onNewIntent` method and add the following code:

```java
@Override
protected void onNewIntent(Intent intent) {
  if (nfcHelper.isNfcIntent(intent)) {
    if (isWritingTag) {

      String text = txtNote.getText().toString();

      NdefMessage ndefMsg = nfcHelper.createTextNdefMessage(text);

      if (nfcHelper.writeNdefMessage(intent, ndefMsg)) {

        Toast.makeText(this, R.string.toast_write_successful,
Toast.LENGTH_LONG).show();
      } else {

        Toast.makeText(this, R.string.toast_write_fail, Toast.
LENGTH_LCNG).show();

      }

      isWritingTag = false;
      writingProgressDialog.dismiss();

    } else {

      // Check Chapter 5 to know how to get tag content

    }
  }

}
```

14. Implement the `handleIntent` method with the following code:

```java
public void handleIntent(Intent intent) {

  String action = intent.getAction();
  String type = intent.getType();
  if (Intent.ACTION_SEND.equals(action) && type != null) {
    if ("text/plain".equals(type)) {
```

```java
        String sharedText = intent.getStringExtra(Intent.EXTRA_
TEXT);
        if (sharedText != null) {
          txtNote.setText(sharedText);
        }
      }
    }
  }
```

15. Implement the `onBtWriteTagClickd` method with the following code:

```java
public void onBtWriteTagClick(View view) {
  String text = txtNote.getText().toString();

  if (text.isEmpty()) {
    Toast.makeText(this, R.string.toast_invalid_note, Toast.
LENGTH_LONG).show();

    return;
  }

  showWaitDialog();
}
```

16. Implement the `showWaitDialog` method with the following code:

```java
private void showWaitDialog() {

  writingProgressDialog = ProgressDialog.show(this, "",
  getString(R.string.dialog_tap_on_tag), false, true, new
  OnCancelListener() {

    @Override
    public void onCancel(DialogInterface arg0) {
      isWritingTag = false;
    }
  });

  isWritingTag = true;

}
```

17. Run the application, type in the note, or share any text with the `NfcBookCh4Note` application. Press the **Write Tag** button.

18. Tap your phone on a tag or simulate a tap in NFC Simulator.

19. A **Write Successful!** toast should appear.

How it works...

In this recipe, we allowed the user to share any plain text to our application. The received shared content is then placed in the `txtNote EditText` view, which allows the user to easily create a note. The content is then written to a tag after the **Write Tag** button is pressed.

Reading Tag Content

In this chapter, we will cover the following topics:

- Obtaining NDEF Message from Intent
- Getting the data out of the message
- Reading a text-formatted record
- Reading a URI-formatted record
- Reading external types
- Reading custom mimes

Introduction

Each tag technology may implement its own standard I/O and depending on that, we may need to implement our own protocol stack on top of the `android.nfc.tech.*` classes. The easiest and more standard way to read NFC tags is by using the NDEF format. In this chapter, we will focus on how to process the different `NdefMessages` types.

Obtaining NDEF Message from Intent

The Android system uses intents to carry data between activities, applications, and events. The same logic is applied in NFC. As we saw in *Chapter 2*, *Detecting a Tag*, the `Tag` instance can be obtained in the intent. The NDEF Messages can also be obtained from there and in this recipe we will see how they can be obtained.

Getting ready

The following settings are required for the recipe:

- Make sure you have a working Android development environment. If you don't, ADT Bundle is a good start (`http://developer.android.com/sdk/index.html`).

- Make sure you have an NFC-enabled Android device or a virtual test environment. Refer to the *Testing your app all together* recipe in *Chapter 1, Getting Started with NFC*.

- It will be assumed that Eclipse is the development IDE.

How to do it...

On performing the following steps, a simple application that allows us to get an NDEF Message from a tag using the intent dispatch system will be created:

1. Open Eclipse and create a new Android application project named `NfcBookCh5Example1` with package name `nfcbook.ch5.example1`.

2. Make sure the `AndroidManifest.xml` file is correctly configured. Refer to the *Requesting NFC permissions* recipe in *Chapter 1, Getting Started with NFC*.

3. Import the `NfcHelper` class into the project and enable the foreground dispatch system by overriding the `onResume` and `onPause` methods:

```java
@Override
protected void onResume() {
  super.onResume();

  if (nfcHelper.isNfcEnabledDevice()) {
    nfcHelper.enableForegroundDispatch();
  }
}

@Override
protected void onPause() {
  super.onPause();

  if (nfcHelper.isNfcEnabledDevice()) {
    nfcHelper.disableForegroundDispatch();
  }
}
```

4. Add the following class member and instantiate it in the `onCreate` method:

```java
private NfcHelper nfcHelper;

protected void onCreate(Bundle savedInstanceState) {
  nfcHelper = new NfcHelper(this);
  ...
}
```

5. Implement the `getNdefMessageFromIntent` method in the `NfcHelper` class:

```java
public NdefMessage getNdefMessageFromIntent(Intent intent) {

    NdefMessage ndefMessage = null;

    Parcelable[] extra = intent.getParcelableArrayExtra(NfcAdapter.
EXTRA_NDEF_MESSAGES);

    if (extra != null && extra.length > 0) {
      ndefMessage = (NdefMessage) extra[0];
    }

    return ndefMessage;

}
```

6. Override the `onNewIntent` method and place the following code:

```java
@Override
protected void onNewIntent(Intent intent) {

    if (nfcHelper.isNfcIntent(intent)) {

      NdefMessage ndefMessage =
        nfcHelper.getNdefMessageFromIntent(intent);

      if (ndefMessage != null) {
        Toast.makeText(this, "Ndef message found!",
          Toast.LENGTH_LONG).show();
      } else {
        Toast.makeText(this, "No Ndef message found.", Toast.LENGTH
_LONG).show();
      }

    }

}
```

7. Run the application and tap on a tag on your phone or simulate a tap in the NFC Simulator on a previously NDEF-formatted tag.

8. A toast should appear indicating if the tag contains an NDEF Message or not.

How it works...

As mentioned in the *Working with the NDEF record* recipe in *Chapter 3, Writing Tag Content*, we can obtain the `Tag` in the intented extras through the `NfcAdapter.EXTRA_TAG` key. To obtain the NDEF Message present in the tag, we use the `NfcAdapter.EXTRA_NDEF_MESSAGES` key. This value is sent in the intent as an array, so we need to call the `getParcelableArrayExtra` method that returns a `Parcelable[]` array. Each object present in the array can then be casted to the `NdefMessage` type.

As stated in the introduction section, we can also get the tag content using the `android.nfc.tech.*` classes, depending on the tag technology. Since we are filtering for the `Ndef` and `NdefFormatable` tags, another way to get `NdefMessage` would be using the following code:

```java
public NdefMessage getNdefMessageFromTag(Tag tag) {
  NdefMessage ndefMessage = null;
  Ndef ndef = Ndef.get(tag);
  if (ndef != null) {
    ndefMessage = ndef.getCachedNdefMessage();
  }
  return ndefMessage;
}
```

The `getCachedNdefMessage` method returns the `NdefMessage` read at tag discovery time so, if we change it, we need to call the `getNdefMessage` method to get the latest message.

Getting the data out of the message

In the previous recipe, we learn how to get `NdefMessage` from the tag, but the actual data is in `NdefRecords` present in the tag. In this recipe, we will see how to get the first `NdefRecord` of `NdefMessage` and how to get its content.

How to do it...

The following steps show how to get the data out of the message:

1. Open Eclipse and create a new Android application project named `NfcBookCh5Example2` and package name `nfcbook.ch5.example2`.

2. Make sure the `AndroidManifest.xml` file is correctly configured. Refer to the *Requesting NFC permissions* recipe in *Chapter 1, Getting Started with NFC*.

3. Import the `NfcHelper` class into the project and enable the foreground dispatch system.

4. Add the following class member and instantiate it in the `onCreate` method:

```java
private NfcHelper nfcHelper;

protected void onCreate(Bundle savedInstanceState) {
  nfcHelper = new NfcHelper(this);
  ...
}
```

5. Implement the `getFirstNdefRecord` method in the `NfcHelper` class using the following code:

```java
public NdefRecord getFirstNdefRecord(NdefMessage
  ndefMessage) {
  NdefRecord ndefRecord = null;
  NdefRecord[] ndefRecords = ndefMessage.getRecords();

  if (ndefRecords != null && ndefRecords.length > 0) {
    ndefRecord = ndefRecords[0];
  }

  return ndefRecord;
}
```

6. Override the `onNewIntent` method and place the following code:

```java
@Override
protected void onNewIntent(Intent intent) {

  if (nfcHelper.isNfcIntent(intent)) {

    NdefMessage ndefMessage =
      nfcHelper.getNdefMessageFromIntent(intent);

    if (ndefMessage != null) {
```

```
        NdefRecord ndefRecord =
          nfcHelper.getFirstNdefRecord(ndefMessage);

        if (ndefRecord != null) {

          Toast.makeText(this, String.format("Ndef record
            found! data length: %s type: %s",
              ndefRecord.getPayload().length,
                ndefRecord.getType()), Toast.LENGTH_LONG)
          .show();

        } else {
          Toast.makeText(this, "No Ndef record found.",
            Toast.LENGTH_LONG).show();
        }
      } else {
        Toast.makeText(this, "No Ndef message found.",
          Toast.LENGTH_LONG).show();
      }


    }


  }
```

7. Run the application and tap on a tag on your phone or simulate a tap in NFC Simulator on a previously NDEF-formatted tag.

8. A toast should appear indicating the data length and the record type.

How it works...

As mentioned in *Chapter 3*, *Writing Tag Content*, an NDEF Message contains one or more `Ndef` records and we can use this feature to write one record containing our data and another record with the AAR record. As Android system uses the first records to determinate the tag type; it's assumed that the first record is the one we want to get the data from. So, in the `getFirstNdefRecord` method, we only return the first record found. Another approach would be iterating every record returned by the `getRecords` method and test each one for its content type. The data itself can be obtained through the `getPayload` method present in the NDEF Message instance. This method returns `byte[]`, which is a raw representation of our data. Depending on the TNF and RTD, we need to have different approaches to handle the data.

Reading a text-formatted record

In this recipe, we will see how to handle the raw payload that we get from `NdefRecord` and `String`.

Getting ready

It will be assumed that Eclipse is the development IDE and you are familiarized creating the text-formatted `NdefRecords`. Refer to the *Writing a text-formatted record* recipe in *Chapter 3, Writing Tag Content*.

How to do it...

This code complements the recipe where we learn how to write a string into a tag. Refer to the *Writing a text-formatted record* recipe in *Chapter 3, Writing Tag Content*.

1. Open Eclipse and create a new Android application project named `NfcBookCh5Example3` with package name `nfcbook.ch5.example3`.

2. Make sure the `AndroidManifest.xml` file is correctly configured. Refer to the *Requesting NFC permissions* recipe in *Chapter 1, Getting Started with NFC*.

3. Import the `NfcHelper` class into the project and enable the foreground dispatch system.

4. Add the following class member and instantiate it in the `onCreate` method:

```java
private NfcHelper nfcHelper;

protected void onCreate(Bundle savedInstanceState) {
  nfcHelper = new NfcHelper(this);
  ...
}
```

5. Implement the `isNdefRecordOfTnfAndRdt` method in the `NfcHelper` class using the following code:

```java
public boolean isNdefRecordOfTnfAndRdt(NdefRecord
  ndefRecord, short tnf, byte[] rdt) {
  return ndefRecord.getTnf() == tnf &&
    Arrays.equals(ndefRecord.getType(), rdt);
}
```

6. Implement the `getTextFromNdefRecord` method in the `NfcHelper` class:

```java
public String getTextFromNdefRecord(NdefRecord ndefRecord)
  {

    String tagContent = null;

    try {

      byte[] payload = ndefRecord.getPayload();

      String textEncoding = ((payload[0] & 128) == 0) ? "UTF-
        8" : "UTF-16";

      int languageSize = payload[0] & 0063;

      tagContent = new String(payload, languageSize + 1,
        payload.length - languageSize - 1, textEncoding);

    } catch (UnsupportedEncodingException e) {
      Log.e("getTextFromNdefRecord", e.getMessage(), e);
    }
    return tagContent;
}
```

7. Override the `onNewIntent` method and place the following code:

```java
@Override
protected void onNewIntent(Intent intent) {

  if (nfcHelper.isNfcIntent(intent)) {

    NdefMessage ndefMsg =
      nfcHelper.getNdefMessageFromIntent(intent);

    if (ndefMsg != null) {

      NdefRecord ndefRecord =
        nfcHelper.getFirstNdefRecord(ndefMsg);

      if (ndefRecord != null) {

        boolean isTextRecord =
          nfcHelper.isNdefRecordOfTnfAndRdt(ndefRecord,
            NdefRecord.TNF_WELL_KNOWN,
              NdefRecord.RTD_TEXT);
```

```java
        if (isTextRecord) {

            String tagContent =
              nfcHelper.getTextFromNdefRecord(ndefRecord);
            Toast.makeText(this, String.format("Content: %s",
              tagContent), Toast.LENGTH_LONG).show();

        } else {
            Toast.makeText(this, "Record is not Text
              formatted.", Toast.LENGTH_LONG).show();
        }

      } else {
        Toast.makeText(this, "No Ndef record found.",
          Toast.LENGTH_LONG).show();
      }

    } else {
      Toast.makeText(this, "No Ndef message found.",
        Toast.LENGTH_LONG).show();
    }

  }

}
```

8. Run the application and tap on a tag on your phone or simulate a tap in NFC Simulator on a previously text NDEF-formatted tag. Refer to the *How to do it...* section of the *Writing a text-formatted record* recipe in *Chapter 3, Writing Tag Content*.

9. A toast should appear indicating the text in the tag.

How it works...

As we saw in the *Writing a text-formatted record* recipe in *Chapter 3, Writing Tag Content*, writing a string requires us to create a byte array, containing the status bit that indicates the text encoding, the language code length, and the string itself. To get a string out of the `byte[]` array, we need to do the exact opposite and break apart the array. We do that in the `getTextFromNdefRecord`. First, we get the language size and determinate the correct encoding to be used. The language information is present in the message because we may need to correctly format the text in the language it was written.

Reading a URI-formatted record

In this recipe, we will see how to obtain a URI from the NDEF record, although the Android system autoprocesses the web URI, and then passes it to the registered URL schemes application. As seen in the *Filtering URI tags* recipe in *Chapter 2, Detecting a Tag*, we can define which URI tags are sent to our application so that we can obtain the URL from the tag, perform something with it, and prevent the default action.

How to do it...

This code complements the *Writing a URI-formatted record* recipe in *Chapter 3, Writing Tag Content*, where we learned how to write a URI into a tag.

1. Open Eclipse and create a new Android application project named `NfcBookCh5Example4` with package name `nfcbook.ch5.example4`.

2. Make sure that the `AndroidManifest.xml` file is correctly configured. Refer to the *Requesting NFC permissions* recipe in *Chapter 1, Getting Started with NFC*.

3. Set the minimum required version to API level 16.

4. Import the `NfcHelper` class into the project and enable the foreground dispatch system.

5. Add the following class member and instantiate it in the onCreate method:

```
private NfcHelper nfcHelper;

protected void onCreate(Bundle savedInstanceState) {
  nfcHelper = new NfcHelper(this);
  ...
}
```

6. Override the `onNewIntent` method and place the following code:

```
@Override
protected void onNewIntent(Intent intent) {

  if (nfcHelper.isNfcIntent(intent)) {

    NdefMessage ndefMsg =
      nfcHelper.getNdefMessageFromIntent(intent);

    if (ndefMsg != null) {

      NdefRecord ndefRecord =
        nfcHelper.getFirstNdefRecord(ndefMsg);
```

```java
    if (ndefRecord != null) {

        boolean isUriRecord =
          nfcHelper.isNdefRecordOfTnfAndRdt(ndefRecord,
            NdefRecord.TNF_WELL_KNOWN, NdefRecord.RTD_URI);
        if (isUriRecord) {

          Uri uri = ndefRecord.toUri();

          startActivity(new Intent(Intent.ACTION_VIEW,
            uri));

        } else {

          Toast.makeText(this, "Record is not URI
            formatted.", Toast.LENGTH_LONG).show();
        }

      } else {
          Toast.makeText(this, "No ndef record found.",
            Toast.LENGTH_LONG).show();
      }

    } else {
      Toast.makeText(this, "No ndef message found.",
        Toast.LENGTH_LONG).show();
    }

  }

}
```

7. Run the application and tap on a tag on your phone or simulate a tap in NFC Simulator on a previous URI-formatted tag.

8. The browser or application that can handle the URI should start.

How it works...

We obtain the URI from the record by calling the `toUri()` method present in the NDEF record instance. To make sure the tag actually contains a URI, we first test the TNF and RDT present in the record. It should match the value of the static fields `NdefRecord.TNF_WELL_KNOWN` and `NdefRecord.RTD_URI`.

> We can also get the URI in the same way we get a string from a tag and parse it to the URI using the `Uri.parse` method. This way, we avoid the need to set the minimum API level to 16.

Reading external types

In this recipe, we will see how we can identify external type formatted tags by testing the RDT value present in the first record with our external type formatted tags in the `domain.name:typename` form.

How to do it...

This code complements the recipe where we learned how to write a URI into a tag. Refer to the *Working with external types* recipe in *Chapter 3, Writing Tag Content*.

1. Open Eclipse and create a new Android application project named `NfcBookCh5Example5` with package name `com.nfcbook.ch5.example65`.

2. Make sure the `AndroidManifest.xml` file is correctly configured. Refer to the *Requesting NFC permissions* recipe in *Chapter 1, Getting Started with NFC*.

3. Import the `NfcHelper` class into the project and enable the foreground dispatch system.

4. Add the following class member and instantiate it in the onCreate method:

```java
private NfcHelper nfcHelper;

protected void onCreate(Bundle savedInstanceState) {
  nfcHelper = new NfcHelper(this);

  ...
}
```

5. Override the `onNewIntent` method and place the following code:

```java
@Override
protected void onNewIntent(Intent intent) {

  if (nfcHelper.isNfcIntent(intent)) {

    NdefMessage ndefMsg =
      nfcHelper.getNdefMessageFromIntent(intent);

    if (ndefMsg != null) {

      NdefRecord ndefRecord =
        nfcHelper.getFirstNdefRecord(ndefMsg);
```

```java
          if (ndefRecord != null) {
            boolean isExternalTypeRecord =
              nfcHelper.isNdefRecordOfTnfAndRdt(ndefRecord,
                NdefRecord.TNF_EXTERNAL_TYPE,
                  "packtpub.com:myexternaltype".getBytes());

            if (isExternalTypeRecord) {

              byte[] payload = ndefRecord.getPayload();

              Toast.makeText(this, String.format("External type
                record found! Payload length: %s", (payload !=
                  null ? payload.length : 0)),
                    Toast.LENGTH_LONG).show();

            } else {

              Toast.makeText(this, "Record is not URI
                formatted.", Toast.LENGTH_LONG).show();
            }

          } else {
            Toast.makeText(this, "No ndef record found.",
              Toast.LENGTH_LONG).show();
          }

        } else {
          Toast.makeText(this, "No ndef message found.",
            Toast.LENGTH_LONG).show();
        }
      }

  }
```

6. Run the application and tap on a tag on your phone or simulate a tap in the NFC Simulator on a previously external type NDEF-formatted tag. Refer to the *Working with external types* recipe in *Chapter 3, Writing Tag Content*.

7. A toast should appear, indicating if any external type record was found.

How it works...

To make sure the tag actually contains any external type formatted record, we test the TNF present in the record with the static value `NdefRecord.TNF_EXTERNAL_TYPE` and the type obtained through the `getType` method with our external type name—`packtpub. com:myexternaltype`. After that, we can get the payload present in the record and handle it. The implementation on how we handle the payload must be according to the writing strategy used because everything depends on what kind of data we have written and how it should be interpreted.

Reading custom mimes

In this recipe, we will see how we can identify tags formatted with our custom mime and how to convert the raw data into an object instance.

How to do it...

The code complements the recipe where we learn how to write a URI into a tag. Refer to the *Working with custom mimes* recipe in *Chapter 3, Writing Tag Content*. Perform the following steps:

1. Open Eclipse and create a new Android application project named `NfcBookCh5Example6` with package name `com.nfcbook.ch5.example6`.

2. Make sure the `AndroidManifest.xml` file is correctly configured. Refer to the *Requesting NFC permissions* recipe in *Chapter 1, Getting Started with NFC*.

3. Set the minimum required version to API level 16.

4. Import `MyClass` from the *Working with custom mimes* recipe in *Chapter 3, Writing Tag Content*.

5. Import the `NfcHelper` class into the project and enable the foreground dispatch system.

6. Add the following class member and instantiate it in the `onCreate` method:

```
private NfcHelper nfcHelper;

protected void onCreate(Bundle savedInstanceState) {
  nfcHelper = new NfcHelper(this);
  . . .
}
```

7. Implement the handle custom mime method using the following code:

```
MyClass handleCustomMime(NdefRecord ndefRecord) {
  byte[] payload = ndefRecord.getPayload();
```

```java
Object o = null;
ByteArrayInputStream bis = new
  ByteArrayInputStream(payload);
ObjectInput in = null;

try {
  in = new ObjectInputStream(bis);
  o = in.readObject();

  bis.close();
  in.close();
} catch (Exception e) {
  Log.e("bytesToObject", e.getMessage());
}

return (MyClass) o;
}
```

8. Override the `onNewIntent` method and place the following code:

```java
@Override
protected void onNewIntent(Intent intent) {

  if (nfcHelper.isNfcIntent(intent)) {

    NdefMessage ndefMsg =
      nfcHelper.getNdefMessageFromIntent(intent);

    if (ndefMsg != null) {

      NdefRecord ndefRecord =
        nfcHelper.getFirstNdefRecord(ndefMsg);

      if (ndefRecord != null) {

        String myCustomMime = "application/vnd." +
          this.getPackageName() + ".MyClass";

        if (ndefRecord.toMimeType().equals(myCustomMime)) {
          Toast.makeText(this,
            handleCustomMime(ndefRecord).toString(),
              Toast.LENGTH_LONG).show();

        } else {
```

```
        Toast.makeText(this, "Record is not formatted in
          our MIME.", Toast.LENGTH_LONG).show();
      }

    } else {
      Toast.makeText(this, "No ndef record found.",
        Toast.LENGTH_LONG).show();
    }
  } else {
    Toast.makeText(this, "No ndef message found.",
      Toast.LENGTH_LONG).show();
  }

}

}
```

9. Run the application and tap on a tag on your phone or simulate a tap in the NFC Simulator on a previously custom mime NDEF-formatted tag.

10. A toast should appear indicating the text in the tag.

How it works...

To make sure the tag actually contains a custom mime record, we test the mime type present in record with our mime. The mime type present in the record can be obtained using the `toMimeType()` method. Then, we desterilize our raw payload into a `MyClass` instance using the `handleCustomMime` method.

6

Reading Tag Content – Real-life Examples

In this chapter, we will cover the following topics:

- Making a phone call with one tap – Part 2
- Sending a predefined SMS – Part 2
- Leaving a (small) note – Part 2
- Getting the tag information

Introduction

In this chapter, we will get a chance to finish the real-life examples we started in *Chapter 4, Writing Tag Content – Real-life Examples*. These simple, yet useful, applications will allow us to see the whole picture and can serve as a base for future and more complex applications.

Making a phone call with one tap – Part 2

In Part 1 of this recipe, we were able to write a phone number to a tag but weren't able to read from the tag. Although the Android system knows how to handle the `tel:*` URI, we may want to prevent the default behavior and handle the tag content ourselves. In this recipe, we will complete the application and create a fully functional application ready for daily use.

Getting ready

- Make sure you have a working Android development environment. If you don't, ADT Bundle is a good kit to start with. It is available at `http://developer.android.com/sdk/index.html`.

- Make sure you have an NFC-enabled Android device or a virtual test environment. Refer to the *Testing your app all together* recipe, in *Chapter 1, Getting Started with NFC*.

- It will be assumed that Eclipse is the development IDE and also that you are familiarized reading Uri formatted NDEF Records. Refer to the *Reading a URI-formatted record* recipe in *Chapter 5, Reading Tag Content*.

- Please have a look at the *Making a phone call with one tap – Part 1* recipe in *Chapter 4, Writing Tag Content – Real-life Examples* first, as we need the result code files to use in this recipe.

How to do it...

In Part 2 of the recipe, we will read the URI in the tag and make a phone call to the saved number. You can jump to step 3 if you have done Part 1 of the recipe and don't want to create a different project.

1. Open Eclipse and create a new Android application project named `NfcBookCh6PhoneCall` and package named `nfcbook.ch6phonecall`.

2. Import the code and resource files from *Chapter 4, Writing Tag Content – Real-life Examples*.

3. Set the minimum required version to API level 16.

4. Request permission to make phone calls by adding the following line of code to the `AndroidManifest.xml` file:

```
<uses-permission
    android:name="android.permission.CALL_PHONE" />
```

5. Implement the `getNdefMessageFromIntent` and the `getFirstNdefRecord` methods from *Chapter 5, Reading Tag Content*, in the `NfcHelper.java` file.

6. Complete the `onNewIntent` method by placing the following code on the `else` part of the `if (isWritingTag)` condition:

```
@Override
protected void onNewIntent(Intent intent) {

    if (nfcHelper.isNfcIntent(intent)) {

        if (isWritingTag) {

            NdefMessage ndefMsg = nfcHelper.createUrlNdefMessage("tel:"
                + txtPhoneNumber.getText().toString());
```

```java
      if (nfcHelper.writeNdefMessage(intent, ndefMsg)) {
        Toast.makeText(this, R.string.toast_write_successful,
          Toast.LENGTH_LONG).show();
      } else {
        Toast.makeText(this, R.string.toast_write_fail,
          Toast.LENGTH_LONG).show();
      }

      isWritingTag = false;
      writingProgressDialog.dismiss();

    } else {

    NdefMessage ndefMessage = nfcHelper.getNdefMessageFromIntent
(intent);

    if (ndefMessage != null) {

      NdefRecord ndefRecord =
        nfcHelper.getFirstNdefRecord(ndefMessage);

      if (ndefRecord != null) {

        Intent callIntent = new Intent(Intent.ACTION_CALL);
        callIntent.setData(ndefRecord.toUri());
        startActivity(callIntent);

      } else {
        Log.i("onNewIntent", "No NdefRecord found.");
      }

    } else {
      Log.i("onNewIntent", "No NdefMessage found.");
    }
     }

    } else {
      handleIntent(intent);
    }
  }
```

7. Run the application and tap your phone on a tag or simulate a tap on NFC Simulator on a previously written tag.

8. A phone call should now be initiated to the number saved in the tag.

How it works...

We used the methods we learned in the previous chapter to get `NdefRecord` out of the tag and then get the saved URI. It should be in the `tel:PHONE_NUMBER` call format so that we can simply start the call activity using the `ACTION_CALL` intent.

The code to read the tag should be only executed when the `isWritingTag` flag is false. This flag helps us control our actions when a tag tap is detected since there are no separate events for these actions.

Sending a predefined SMS – Part 2

In Part 1 of this recipe, we were able to write a phone number and the SMS content to a tag, but we didn't implement the logic to read it. In this recipe, we will complete the application and create a fully functional application ready for daily use.

Getting ready

Please have a look at the *Sending a predefined SMS – Part 1* recipe in *Chapter 4, Writing Tag Content – Real-life Examples* first, as we need to use the result code files in this recipe.

How to do it...

In Part 2 of the recipe, we will read the URI in the tag and send an SMS. You can jump to step three if you have done Part 1 of the recipe and don't want to create a different project.

1. Open Eclipse and create a new Android application project named `NfcBookCh6Sms` and a package named `nfcbook.ch6sms`.

2. Import the code and resources files from the *Sending a predefined SMS – Part 1* recipe in *Chapter 4, Writing Tag Content – Real-life Examples*.

3. With the following code, request permissions to send an SMS:

   ```xml
   <uses-permission android:name="android.permission.SEND_SMS" />
   ```

4. Set the minimum required version to API level 16.

5. Implement the `getNdefMessageFromIntent` and `getFirstNdefRecord` methods from *Chapter 5, Reading Tag Content*, in the `NfcHelper.java` file.

6. Implement the `sendSms` method with the following code:

```
private void sendSms(final String phoneNumber, final String
message) {

    AlertDialog.Builder builder = new AlertDialog.Builder(this);

    builder.setTitle("Send SMS");
    builder.setMessage(String.format("do you want to send an SMS to
      %s?", phoneNumber));

    builder.setPositiveButton(android.R.string.yes, new
      DialogInterface.OnClickListener() {

      public void onClick(DialogInterface dialog, int which) {

        // send SMS!
        SmsManager smsManager = SmsManager.getDefault();
        smsManager.sendTextMessage(phoneNumber, null, message, null,
          null);

        dialog.dismiss();
      }

    });

    builder.setNegativeButton(android.R.string.no, null);

    AlertDialog alert = builder.create();

    alert.show();

}
```

7. Complete the `onNewIntent` method with the following code:

```
@Override
protected void onNewIntent(Intent intent) {

    if (nfcHelper.isNfcIntent(intent)) {
      if (isWritingTag) {

        String smsUri = String.format("sms:%s?body=%s",
          txtPhoneNumber.getText().toString(), URLEncoder.
encode(txtSmsBody.getText().toString()));
```

```java
            NdefMessage ndefMsg =
              nfcHelper.createUrlNdefMessage(smsUri);

            if (nfcHelper.writeNdefMessage(intent, ndefMsg)) {

              Toast.makeText(this, R.string.toast_write_successful,
                Toast.LENGTH_LONG).show();
            } else {

              Toast.makeText(this, R.string.toast_write_fail,
                Toast.LENGTH_LONG).show();

            }

            isWritingTag = false;
            writingProgressDialog.dismiss();

        } else {

          NdefMessage ndefMessage =
            nfcHelper.getNdefMessageFromIntent(intent);

          if (ndefMessage != null) {

            NdefRecord ndefRecord =
              nfcHelper.getFirstNdefRecord(ndefMessage);

            if (ndefRecord != null) {

              String[] smsUriParts =
                ndefRecord.toUri().getSchemeSpecificPart().
                  split("\\?body=");

              sendSms(smsUriParts[0], smsUriParts[1]);

            } else {
              Log.i("onNewIntent", "No NdefRecord found.");
            }

          } else {
            Log.i("onNewIntent", "No NdefMessage found.");
          }
```

```
    }
  } else {
    handleIntent(intent);
  }

}
```

8. Run the application and tap your phone on a tag or simulate a tap in NFC Simulator on a previously written tag.

9. A dialog will appear that will ask you whether you wish to send the SMS.

How it works...

We used the methods learned in the previous chapters to get `NdefRecord` out of the tag and then get the saved URI using the `toUri` method in the record. It should be in SMS format, that is, `sms:PHONE_NUMBER?body=SMS_BODY` so that we can break it apart and get the destination number and the message body and use `SmsManager` to send the message.

The code to read the tag should be only executed when the `isWritingTag` flag is false. This flag helps us control our actions when a tag tap is detected since there are no separate events for these actions.

Leaving a (small) note – Part 2

In the Part 1 of this recipe, we were able to write a small note to a tag, but when we tapped the phone on the written tag, the application started but no content was displayed. In this recipe, we will complete the application by implementing the read tag content logic.

Getting ready

First, have a look at the *Leaving a (small) note – Part 1* recipe in *Chapter 4, Writing Tag Content – Real-life Examples*, as we need to use the result code files in this recipe.

How to do it...

In Part 2 of the recipe, we will read the text in the tag and place it in `EditText`. You can jump to step 5 if you have done Part 1 of the recipe and don't want to create a different project.

1. Open Eclipse and create a new Android application project named `NfcBookCh6Note` and package named `nfcbook.ch6note`.

2. Import the code and resources files from the *Leaving a (small) note – Part 1* recipe in *Chapter 4, Writing Tag Content – Real-life Examples*.

3. Implement the `getNdefMessageFromIntent` and the `getFirstNdefRecord` methods from *Chapter 5, Reading Tag Content*, in `NfcHelper.java`

4. Implement the `getTextFromNdefRecord` method in the `NfcHelper` class:

```java
public String getTextFromNdefRecord(NdefRecord ndefRecord) {

    String tagContent = null;

    try {

      byte[] payload = ndefRecord.getPayload();

      String textEncoding = ((payload[0] & 128) == 0) ? "UTF-8" :
"UTF-16";

      int languageSize = payload[0] & 0063;

      tagContent = new String(payload, languageSize + 1, payload.
length - languageSize - 1, textEncoding);

    } catch (UnsupportedEncodingException e) {

      Log.e("getTextFromNdefRecord", e.getMessage(), e);

    }

    return tagContent;

  }
```

5. Replace the `onNewIntent` method with the following code:

```java
@Override
protected void onNewIntent(Intent intent) {

  if (nfcHelper.isNfcIntent(intent)) {
    if (isWritingTag) {

      String text = txtNote.getText().toString();

      NdefMessage ndefMsg = nfcHelper.createTextNdefMessage(text);

      if (nfcHelper.writeNdefMessage(intent, ndefMsg)) {

        Toast.makeText(this, R.string.toast_write_successful,
          Toast.LENGTH_LONG).show();
      } else {

        Toast.makeText(this, R.string.toast_write_fail,
          Toast.LENGTH_LONG).show();
```

```
            }

            isWritingTag = false;
            writingProgressDialog.dismiss();

        } else {
          NdefMessage ndefMessage =
            nfcHelper.getNdefMessageFromIntent(intent);

          if (ndefMessage != null) {

            NdefRecord ndefRecord =
              nfcHelper.getFirstNdefRecord(ndefMessage);

            if (ndefRecord != null) {
              String text = nfcHelper.getTextFromNdefRecord
                (ndefRecord);

              txtNote.setText(text);
            } else {
              Log.i("onNewIntent", "No NdefRecord found.");
            }

          } else {
            Log.i("onNewIntent", "No NdefMessage found.");
          }

        }
      }

    }
```

6. Run the application and tap your phone on a tag or simulate a tap in NFC Simulator on a previously written tag.

7. The activity should start and the tag content will be displayed in the main `EditText` view.

How it works...

We used the methods we learned in the previous chapter to get `NdefRecord` out of the tag and then get the saved text content and fill the textbox with it.

The code for reading the tag should be executed only when the `isWritingTag` flag is false. This flag helps us control our actions when a tag tap is detected since there are no separate events for these actions.

Getting the tag information

In this recipe, we will see how to obtain several types of information regarding an NFC tag and its content.

How to do it...

We will get the tag information through the `Tag` object instance, and the information regarding its content will be based on the first `NdefRecord` present in the tag.

1. Open Eclipse and create a new Android application project named `NfcBookCh7Example1` and package named `com.nfcbook.ch7.example1`.

2. Make sure the `AndroidManifest.xml` file is configured correctly. Refer to the *Requesting NFC permissions* recipe in *Chapter 1, Getting Started with NFC*.

3. Add the following `intent-filter` to `MainActivity`:

```xml
<intent-filter>
  <action android:name="android.nfc.action.NDEF_DISCOVERED"
    />

  <category android:name="android.intent.category.DEFAULT"
    />

  <data android:mimeType="text/plain" />
</intent-filter>
```

4. Add the following content to the `strings.xml` file located at `/res/values`:

```xml
<string name="title_activity_tag_details">Tag Details</string>
<string name="tag_type">Type</string>
<string name="tag_id">Id</string>
<string name="tag_content_type">Content Type</string>
<string name="tag_content_length">Content Length</string>
<string name="tag_content">Content</string>
```

5. Replace the content of the `activity_main.xml` file located at `/res/layout` with the following code:

```xml
<RelativeLayout xmlns:android="http://schemas.android.com/apk/res/
android"
    xmlns:tools="http://schemas.android.com/tools"
    android:layout_width="match_parent"
    android:layout_height="match_parent"
    android:paddingBottom="@dimen/activity_vertical_margin"
```

```xml
    android:paddingLeft="@dimen/activity_horizontal_margin"
    android:paddingRight=
      "@dimen/activity_horizontal_margin"
    android:paddingTop="@dimen/activity_vertical_margin"
    tools:context=".TagDetailsActivity" >
    <TextView
        android:id="@+id/textView1"
        android:layout_width="wrap_content"
        android:layout_height="wrap_content"
        android:layout_alignParentLeft="true"
        android:layout_alignParentTop="true"
        android:text="@string/tag_id"
        android:textAppearance=
          "?android:attr/textAppearanceMedium" />

    <TextView
        android:id="@+id/txtViewTagId"
        android:layout_width="wrap_content"
        android:layout_height="wrap_content"
        android:layout_alignLeft="@+id/textView1"
        android:layout_below="@+id/textView1"
        android:text=""
        android:textAppearance=
          "?android:attr/textAppearanceSmall" />

    <TextView
        android:id="@+id/textView2"
        android:layout_width="wrap_content"
        android:layout_height="wrap_content"
        android:layout_alignLeft="@+id/txtViewTagId"
        android:layout_below="@+id/txtViewTagId"
        android:layout_marginTop="10dp"
        android:text="@string/tag_type"
        android:textAppearance=
          "?android:attr/textAppearanceMedium" />

    <TextView
        android:id="@+id/txtViewTagType"
        android:layout_width="wrap_content"
        android:layout_height="wrap_content"
        android:layout_alignLeft="@+id/textView2"
        android:layout_below="@+id/textView2"
        android:text=""
```

```xml
        android:textAppearance=
            "?android:attr/textAppearanceSmall" />

    <TextView
        android:id="@+id/txtViewTagContentType"
        android:layout_width="wrap_content"
        android:layout_height="wrap_content"
        android:layout_alignParentLeft="true"
        android:layout_below="@+id/TextView02"
        android:text=""
        android:textAppearance=
            "?android:attr/textAppearanceSmall" />

    <TextView
        android:id="@+id/TextView02"
        android:layout_width="wrap_content"
        android:layout_height="wrap_content"
        android:layout_alignLeft="@+id/txtViewTagType"
        android:layout_below="@+id/txtViewTagType"
        android:layout_marginTop="10dp"
        android:text="@string/tag_content_type"
        android:textAppearance=
            "?android:attr/textAppearanceMedium" />

    <TextView
        android:id="@+id/txtViewTagContentLength"
        android:layout_width="wrap_content"
        android:layout_height="wrap_content"
        android:layout_alignParentLeft="true"
        android:layout_below="@+id/TextView03"
        android:text=""
        android:textAppearance=
            "?android:attr/textAppearanceSmall" />

    <TextView
        android:id="@+id/TextView03"
        android:layout_width="wrap_content"
        android:layout_height="wrap_content"
        android:layout_alignLeft=
            "@+id/txtViewTagContentType"
        android:layout_below="@+id/txtViewTagContentType"
        android:layout_marginTop="10dp"
        android:text="@string/tag_content_length"
        android:textAppearance=
            "?android:attr/textAppearanceMedium" />
    <TextView
        android:id="@+id/TextView05"
```

```xml
        android:layout_width="wrap_content"
        android:layout_height="wrap_content"
        android:layout_alignLeft=
          "@+id/txtViewTagContentLength"
        android:layout_below="@+id/txtViewTagContentLength"
        android:layout_marginTop="10dp"
        android:text="@string/tag_content"
        android:textAppearance=
          "?android:attr/textAppearanceMedium" />

    <EditText
        android:id="@+id/edTextContent"
        android:layout_width="wrap_content"
        android:layout_height="wrap_content"
        android:layout_alignLeft="@+id/TextView05"
        android:layout_alignParentBottom="true"
        android:layout_alignParentRight="true"
        android:layout_below="@+id/TextView05"
        android:ems="10"
        android:enabled="false"
        android:inputType="text"  >

        <requestFocus />
    </EditText>
</RelativeLayout>
```

6. The preceding code creates a layout which should be identical to the following screenshot:

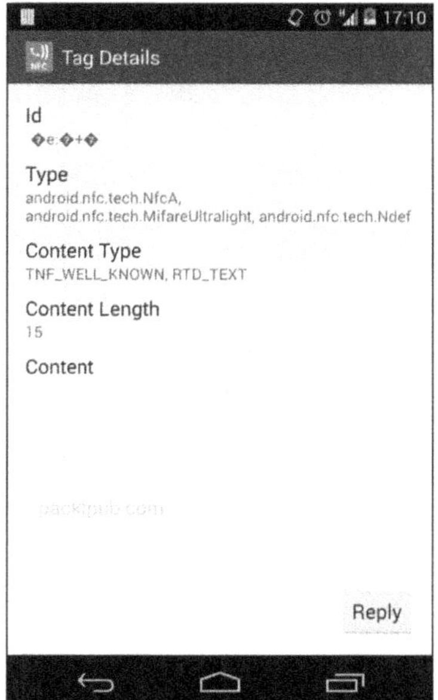

7. Import the `NfcHelper` class to the project and enable the foreground dispatch system.

8. Open `MainActivity` and add the following class members:

```java
NfcHelper nfcHelper;
EditText edTextContent;
TextView txtViewTagId;
TextView txtViewTagType;
TextView txtViewTagContentType;
TextView txtViewTagContentLength;
```

9. Replace the `onCreate` method:

```java
@Override
protected void onCreate(Bundle savedInstanceState) {
  super.onCreate(savedInstanceState);
  setContentView(R.layout.activity_main);

  nfcHelper = new NfcHelper(this);

  edTextContent = ((EditText) findViewById(R.id.edTextContent));

  txtViewTagId = ((TextView) findViewById(R.id.txtViewTagId));

  txtViewTagType = ((TextView) findViewById(R.id.txtViewTagType));

  txtViewTagContentType = ((TextView)
    findViewById(R.id.txtViewTagContentType));

  txtViewTagContentLength = ((TextView)
    findViewById(R.id.txtViewTagContentLength));

  if (nfcHelper.isNfcIntent(getIntent())) {
    handleNfcIntent(getIntent());
  }

}
```

10. Implement the `tnfToString` method:

```java
private String tnfToString(short tnf) {

  switch (tnf) {
  case NdefRecord.TNF_EMPTY:
```

```java
      return "TNF_EMPTY";
    case NdefRecord.TNF_ABSOLUTE_URI:

      return "TNF_ABSOLUTE_URI";
    case NdefRecord.TNF_EXTERNAL_TYPE:

      return "TNF_EXTERNAL_TYPE";
    case NdefRecord.TNF_MIME_MEDIA:

      return "TNF_MIME_MEDIA";
    case NdefRecord.TNF_UNCHANGED:

      return "TNF_UNCHANGED";

    case NdefRecord.TNF_WELL_KNOWN:

      return "TNF_WELL_KNOWN";
    default:
    case NdefRecord.TNF_UNKNOWN:

      return "TNF_UNKNOWN";
    }
  }
```

11. Implement the `rtdToString` method:

```java
private String rtdToString(byte[] rdt) {

    if (Arrays.equals(rdt, NdefRecord.RTD_ALTERNATIVE_CARRIER)) {
      return "RTD_ALTERNATIVE_CARRIER";

    } else if (Arrays.equals(rdt, NdefRecord.RTD_HANDOVER_CARRIER))
      {
      return "RTD_HANDOVER_CARRIER";

    } else if (Arrays.equals(rdt, NdefRecord.RTD_HANDOVER_REQUEST))
{
      return "RTD_HANDOVER_REQUEST";

    } else if (Arrays.equals(rdt, NdefRecord.RTD_HANDOVER_SELECT)) {
      return "RTD_HANDOVER_SELECT";

    } else if (Arrays.equals(rdt, NdefRecord.RTD_SMART_POSTER)) {
      return "RTD_SMART_POSTER";
```

```java
    } else if (Arrays.equals(rdt, NdefRecord.RTD_TEXT)) {
      return "RTD_TEXT";

    } else if (Arrays.equals(rdt, NdefRecord.RTD_URI)) {
      return "RTD_URI";

    } else {
      return "RTD_UNKNOWN";
    }

  }
```

12. Implement the `handleNfcIntent` method:

```java
void handleNfcIntent(Intent intent) {

    Tag tag = nfcHelper.getTagFromIntent(intent);
    NdefMessage ndefMessage = nfcHelper.getNdefMessageFromIntent(int
ent);

    if (ndefMessage != null) {

      NdefRecord ndefRecord =
        nfcHelper.getFirstNdefRecord(ndefMessage);

      if (ndefRecord != null) {

        String content = nfcHelper.
          getTextFromNdefRecord(ndefRecord);
        String tnf = tnfToString(ndefRecord.getTnf());
        String rtd = rtdToString(ndefRecord.getType());

        edTextContent.setText(content);

        txtViewTagId.setText(Base64.encodeToString(tag.getId(),
          Base64.DEFAULT));

        txtViewTagType.setText(TextUtils.join(", ",
          tag.getTechList()));

        txtViewTagContentType.setText(tnf + ", " + rtd);

        txtViewTagContentLength.setText("" +
          ndefRecord.getPayload().length);

      }
```

```
    }

}
```

13. Override the `onNewIntent` method:

```
@Override
protected void onNewIntent(Intent intent) {

  if (nfcHelper.isNfcIntent(intent)) {
    handleNfcIntent(intent);
  }
}
```

14. Run the application and tap your phone on a tag or simulate a tap in NFC Simulator on a previously written tag.

15. The activity will start and information about the tag and its content should be displayed.

How it works...

This application will allow us to get an insight on an NDEF-formatted tag. It displays information such as the tag's unique identifier and its type. We also use the first `NdefRecord` parameter present in `NdefMessage` along with its TNF and RTD as well as the payload length and a string representation of it. This is useful because it allows us to know whether we are formatting a tag correctly or just to know what is inside the tag.

7

Sharing Content across Devices

In this chapter, we will cover the following topics:

- Creating a basic peer-to-peer Hello World application
- Sending texts to other devices
- Sending a friend invite on Facebook
- Inviting a friend to play a game – Part 1

Introduction

The Android system provides an NFC functionality called **Android Beam**. This functionality allows users to use NFC not only to read and write tags, but also to share content directly between devices. By default, it allows users to share URLs, contacts, and applications (not really the `.apk` file but at the Play Store address at `https://play.google.com/store/apps/details?id=APP_ID`). This is a great tool for users to interact with other users and easily share content between them. There is no faster way for sharing URLs or contacts than this way! In this chapter, we will learn how to use it.

Android Beam is just a cool name for the Android feature that uses **Simple NDEF Exchange Protocol** (**SNEP**). This protocol is defined by the NFC Forum and allows an NFC-enabled device to exchange NDEF messages with another NFC Forum device while operating in the peer-to-peer mode. SNEP is built on top of the NFC **Logical Link Control Protocol** (**LLCP**) that defines an OSI layer-2 protocol to support peer-to-peer communication between two NFC-enabled devices. These protocols allow Android and non-Android devices to exchange data through NFC.

By default, Android Beam tries to use SNEP first, and if that fails, it tries the Android **NDEF Push Protocol** (**NPP**), which is also built on top of LLCP.

Creating a basic peer-to-peer Hello World application

In this recipe, we will create a simple project that allows us to understand the basics of the Android Beam functionality and what we need to do to make it work. The knowledge acquired in this recipe will be used in each of the rest of the recipes in this chapter.

Getting ready

We need the following settings for this recipe:

- Make sure you have a working Android development environment. If you don't, ADT Bundle is a good kit to start with. You can download it from `http://developer.android.com/sdk/index.html`.

- Make sure you have an NFC-enabled Android device or a virtual test environment—refer to the *Testing your app all together* recipe in *Chapter 1, Getting Started with NFC*.

- It will be assumed that Eclipse is the development IDE.

How to do it...

In this application, we will send an empty `NdefMessage` parameter to the other device and display a toast to indicate that we sent as well as received the message correctly, as shown in the following steps:

1. Open Eclipse and create a new Android application project named `NfcBookCh7Example1` and a package named `nfcbook.ch7.example1`.

2. Make sure the `AndroidManifest.xml` file is configured correctly—refer to the *Requesting NFC permissions* recipe in *Chapter 1, Getting Started with NFC*.

3. Set the minimum SDK version to `16` with the following code:

```
<uses-sdk android:minSdkVersion="16" />
```

4. Add the following `intent-filter` object to `MainActivity` in the `AndroidManifest` file:

```
<intent-filter>
  <action android:name="android.nfc.action.NDEF_DISCOVERED" />

  <category android:name="android.intent.category.DEFAULT" />

  <data
    android:host="ext"
```

```
    android:pathPrefix="/com.packtpub:ch7example1type"
    android:scheme="vnd.android.nfc" />
</intent-filter>
```

5. Import the `NfcHelper` class into the project.

6. Implement the `CreateMimeNdefMessage` method in the `NfcHelper` class with the following code:

```
public NdefMessage createExternalTypeNdefMessage(String type,
byte[] data) {

  NdefRecord externalRecord = NdefRecord.createExternal("com.
packtpub", type, data);

  NdefMessage ndefMessage = new NdefMessage(new NdefRecord[] {
externalRecord });

  return ndefMessage;
}
```

7. Add the following class members and instantiate them in the `onCreate` method:

```
private NfcHelper nfcHelper;
private Handler handler;

@Override
protected void onCreate(Bundle savedInstanceState) {
  super.onCreate(savedInstanceState);
  setContentView(R.layout.activity_main);

  nfcHelper = new NfcHelper(this);

  handler = new Handler() {
    @Override
    public void handleMessage(Message msg) {

      Toast.makeText(getApplicationContext(), "Beam sent!", Toast.
LENGTH_LONG).show();

    }
  };

}
```

We need to use a `Handler` class—`developer.android.com/reference/android/os/Handler.html`—to show a toast to the user when the operation is complete because the call back method does not run on a UI thread.

8. Implement the following `CreateNdefMessageCallback` interface and the corresponding `createNdefMessage` method in `MainActivity`:

```
public class MainActivity extends Activity implements
    CreateNdefMessageCallback {

    ...


    @Override
    public NdefMessage createNdefMessage(NfcEvent event) {
      return nfcHelper.createExternalTypeNdefMessage("ch7example1ty
    pe", new byte[0]);
    }
```

9. Implement the following `OnNdefPushCompleteCallback` interface and the corresponding `onNdefPushComplete` method in `MainActivity`:

```
public class MainActivity extends Activity implements
    CreateNdefMessageCallback, OnNdefPushCompleteCallback {

    ...


    @Override
    public void onNdefPushComplete(NfcEvent event) {
      handler.obtainMessage(1).sendToTarget();
    }


}
```

10. Enable the `NdefPush` interface on `MainActivity` by adding the following lines of code in the `onCreate` method:

```
protected void onCreate(Bundle savedInstanceState) {


    ...


    NfcAdapter nfcAdapter = NfcAdapter.getDefaultAdapter(this);

    nfcAdapter.setNdefPushMessageCallback(this, this);
    nfcAdapter.setOnNdefPushCompleteCallback(this, this);


}
```

11. Override the `onNewIntent` method and insert the following code:

```
@Override
public vcid onNewIntent(Intent intent) {
  setIntent(intent);
}
```

12. Override the `onResume` method and insert the following code:

```
@Override
protected void onResume() {

super.onResume();
if (!nfcHelper.isNfcIntent(getIntent())) {
    return;
  }

  Toast.makeText(this, "Beam received!", Toast.LENGTH_LONG).
show();
}
```

13. Run the application on two smartphones and bring them close with their backs facing each other.

14. The following **Touch to beam** message will appear:

15. Tap on one of the devices to send `NdefMessage` to the other.

16. A **Beam sent!** toast should appear on the device that has been touched and a **Beam received!** toast should appear in the other device.

If you don't have two NFC-enabled devices for testing, you can still use the virtual testing environment that we set up in the *Configuring the Connection Center tool* recipe in *Chapter 1, Getting Started with NFC*. To use it, we need to start two different AVDs, and then in NFC Controller Simulator, choose **NFC Device #2** to simulate the tap of the devices.

How it works...

To enable our `MainActivity` to push NDEF messages to other devices, we must implement the `CreateNdefMessageCallback` and `OnNdefPushCompleteCallback` interfaces that require us to implement the `createNdefMessage` and `onNdefPushComplete` methods, respectively. The first one gets called when the user touches the **Touch to beam** message that appears when the devices get close enough to initiate the content share. The second one gets called when `NdefPush` is complete. In this method, we use a handler to show the toast because it runs on a non-UI thread.

We also need to register our `MainActivity` to push NDEF messages so that when we tap both devices, the default mechanism doesn't start. To do that, we register `MainActivity` as `NdefPushMessageCallback` and `NdefPushCompleteCallback` by calling the `setNdefPushMessageCallback()` and `setOnNdefPushCompleteCallback()` methods from `NfcAdapter`. Note that if we don't configure our `MainActivity` to push NDEF messages correctly, the Android system will still beam an AAR to either start the application on the other end or to go to Play Store to get the application.

Finally, we need to handle the NFC intent started by the system while we receive the pushed `NdefMessage` parameter. This works in the same way as tag reading.

Sending texts to other devices

Android Beam uses the standard `NdefMessage` parameter to share data between devices, and as we learned in *Chapter 3, Writing Tag Content*, we can encapsulate the text to `NdefMessage`. In this recipe, we will create a simple application that sends texts to other devices.

How to do it...

In this application, we will send the content of `TextView` to another device through an `NdefMessage`, which is formatted as `RTD_TEXT`, as shown in the following steps:

1. Open Eclipse and create a new Android application project named `NfcBookCh7Example2` and a package named `nfcbook.ch7.example2`.

2. Make sure the `AndroidManifest.xml` file is configured correctly. Refer to the *Requesting NFC permissions* recipe in *Chapter 1, Getting Started with NFC*.

3. Set the minimum SDK version to `14` with the following code:

```
<uses-sdk android:minSdkVersion="14" />
```

4. Add the following `intent-filters` to `MainActivity` in the `AndroidManifest` file:

```
<intent-filter>
  <action android:name="android.nfc.action.NDEF_DISCOVERED" />
    <category android:name="android.intent.category.DEFAULT" />
    <data android:mimeType="*/*" />
</intent-filter>
<intent-filter>
  <action android:name="android.intent.action.SEND" />

  <category android:name="android.intent.category.DEFAULT" />

  <data android:mimeType="text/plain" />
</intent-filter>
```

5. Replace the content of the `activity_main.xml` file located at `/res/layout` with the following code:

```
<RelativeLayout xmlns:android="http://schemas.android.com/apk/res/
android"
    xmlns:tools="http://schemas.android.com/tools"
    android:layout_width="match_parent"
    android:layout_height="match_parent"
    android:paddingBottom="@dimen/activity_vertical_margin"
    android:paddingLeft="@dimen/activity_horizontal_margin"
    android:paddingRight="@dimen/activity_horizontal_margin"
    android:paddingTop="@dimen/activity_vertical_margin"
    tools:context=".MainActivity" >

    <EditText
        android:id="@+id/edtTextToSend"
        android:layout_width="wrap_content"
        android:layout_height="wrap_content"
        android:layout_above="@+id/textView1"
        android:layout_alignParentLeft="true"
        android:layout_alignParentRight="true"
        android:layout_alignParentTop="true"
        android:ems="10"
        android:inputType="textMultiLine" >
```

```
            <requestFocus />
        </EditText>

        <TextView
            android:id="@+id/textView1"
            android:layout_width="wrap_content"
            android:layout_height="wrap_content"
            android:layout_alignParentBottom="true"
            android:layout_alignParentLeft="true"
            android:layout_alignParentRight="true"
            android:gravity="center"
            android:text="bring both devices close to send the text!"
    />


    </RelativeLayout>
```

The previous code creates a layout that is identical to the following screenshot:

6. Import the `NfcHelper` class onto the project.

7. Follow the steps from 7 to 11 from the previous recipe to enable NDEF push on `MainActivity`.

8. Replace the `createNdefMessage` method with the following code:

```java
@Override
public NdefMessage createNdefMessage(NfcEvent event) {

    String content = ((TextView) findViewById(R.id.edtTextToSend)).
getText().toString();

    return new NdefMessage( new NdefRecord[]{ nfcHelper.
createTextRecord(content)  }

}
```

9. Implement the `handleIntent` method with the following code:

```java
private void handleIntent(Intent intent) {

    if (!nfcHelper.isNfcIntent(intent)) {

        String action = intent.getAction();
        String type = intent.getType();

        if (Intent.ACTION_SEND.equals(action) && type != null) {
            if ("text/plain".equals(type)) {

                String sharedText = intent.getStringExtra(Intent.EXTRA_
TEXT);

                if (sharedText != null) {
                    ((TextView) findViewById(R.id.edtTextToSend)).
setText(sharedText);
                }

            }
        }

        return;
    }

    NdefMessage ndefMessage = nfcHelper.getNdefMessageFromIntent(int
ent);
    NdefRecord ndefRecord = nfcHelper.getFirstNdefRecord(ndefMessa
ge);
```

```java
String text = nfcHelper.getTextFromNdefRecord(ndefRecord);

Toast.makeText(this, text, Toast.LENGTH_LONG).show();
}
```

10. Override the `onResume` method and insert the following code:

```java
@Override
protected void onResume() {
super.onResume();
handleIntent(getIntent());
}
```

11. Run the application on two smartphones, write some text, and bring them close with their backs facing each other. Tap on one of the devices to send `NdefMessage` to the other.

12. A **Beam sent!** toast should appear in the device that is touched, and the written text should appear in the other device.

How it works...

This recipe tries to demonstrate how we can use the peer-to-peer mechanism to share a text-formatted message, testing the fact that we can still use any of the previously learned NDEF message types. The type of the message will influence how we filter the intent in the `handleIntent` method and how we read the tag content.

If we return `null` or an empty message, the Android system will not trigger any event.

Sending a friend invite on Facebook

Social networks allow us to interact with our friends and the world as they are getting increasingly globalized. NFC can also play its part in social networking by facilitating and improving the user's experience. In this recipe, we will see how the NFC technology can bring people closer by simplifying the process of initiating friend requests on Facebook.

Getting ready

We need the following settings for this recipe:

- We will need two active Facebook accounts. One account should be a part of the developer program.

- The Facebook application needs to be installed on the emulators (you can learn how to do this by navigating to `https://developers.facebook.com/docs/android/getting-started/#install`) or on the smartphones, and each one should be signed in with a different account.

How to do it...

In this application, we will send a Facebook friend request with an NDEF message by performing the following steps:

1. Download the Facebook SDK for Android from `https://developers.facebook.com/docs/android/downloads` and import the project to the Eclipse workspace.

2. Open Eclipse and create a new Android application project named `NfcBookCh7Example3` and a package named `nfcbook.ch7.example3`.

3. Open the project's properties window, go to the **Android** option on the left, and click on **Add** in the library section. Add **FacebookSDK** as a library reference, as shown in the following screenshot:

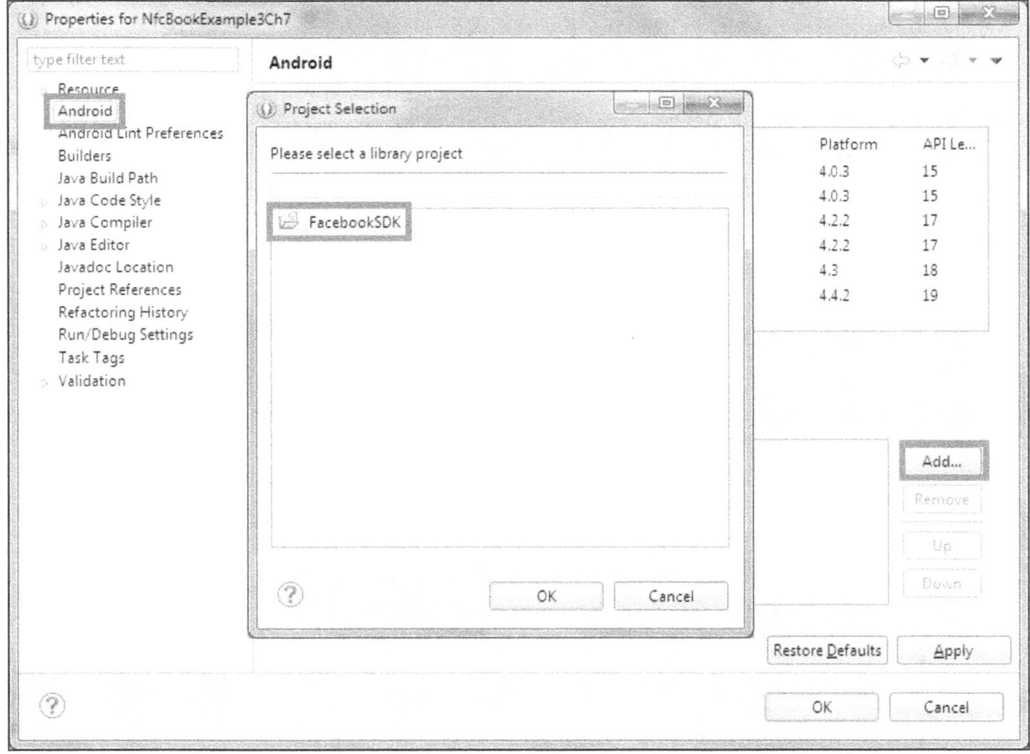

4. Make sure the `AndroidManifest.xml` file is configured correctly —refer to the *Requesting NFC permissions* recipe in *Chapter 1, Getting Started with NFC*.

5. Set the minimum SDK version to `16` with the following code:

```
<uses-sdk android:minSdkVersion="16" />
```

6. Add the following `intent-filter` object to `MainActivity` in the `AndroidManifest` file:

```xml
<intent-filter>
    <action android:name="android.nfc.action.NDEF_DISCOVERED" />

    <category android:name="android.intent.category.DEFAULT" />

    <data
        android:host="ext"
        android:pathPrefix="/com.packtpub:ch7example3type"
        android:scheme="vnd.android.nfc" />
</intent-filter>
```

7. Add the following string definition to the `strings.xml` file located at `/res/values` and replace `MY_APP_ID` for your Facebook application ID:

```xml
<string name="app_id">MY_APP_ID</string>
```

8. Replace the content of the `activity_main.xml` file located at `/res/layout` with the following code:

```xml
<RelativeLayout xmlns:android="http://schemas.android.com/apk/res/android"
    xmlns:tools="http://schemas.android.com/tools"
    xmlns:app="http://schemas.android.com/apk/res-auto"
    android:layout_width="match_parent"
    android:layout_height="match_parent"
    android:paddingBottom="@dimen/activity_vertical_margin"
    android:paddingLeft="@dimen/activity_horizontal_margin"
    android:paddingRight="@dimen/activity_horizontal_margin"
    android:paddingTop="@dimen/activity_vertical_margin"
    tools:context=".MainActivity" >

    <com.facebook.widget.ProfilePictureView
        android:id="@+id/profilePicture"
        android:layout_width="wrap_content"
        android:layout_height="wrap_content"
        android:layout_alignParentLeft="true"
        android:layout_alignParentTop="true"
        android:gravity="center_horizontal"
        app:preset_size="normal" >
    </com.facebook.widget.ProfilePictureView>

    <TextView
        android:id="@+id/txtUserId"
```

```xml
        android:layout_width="wrap_content"
        android:layout_height="wrap_content"
        android:layout_alignBottom="@+id/profilePicture"
        android:layout_alignLeft="@+id/txtUserName"
        android:layout_alignParentRight="true"
        android:text=""
        android:textAppearance="?android:attr/textAppearanceSmall"
    />

    <TextView
        android:id="@+id/txtUserName"
        android:layout_width="wrap_content"
        android:layout_height="wrap_content"
        android:layout_above="@+id/txtUserId"
        android:layout_alignParentRight="true"
        android:layout_toRightOf="@+id/profilePicture"
        android:layout_marginLeft="25dip"
        android:text=""
        android:textAppearance="?android:attr/
textAppearanceMedium" />

    <TextView
        android:id="@+id/textView1"
        android:layout_width="wrap_content"
        android:layout_height="wrap_content"
        android:layout_above="@+id/txtUserName"
        android:layout_alignLeft="@+id/txtUserName"
        android:layout_alignRight="@+id/txtUserName"
        android:text="Hello, " />

</RelativeLayout>
```

The previous code creates a layout that is identical to the following screenshot:

9. Add the following `meta-data` and `activity` definitions to `MainActivity` in the `AndroidManifest` file:

```xml
<meta-data
    android:name="com.facebook.sdk.ApplicationId"
    android:value="@string/app_id" />

<activity android:name="com.facebook.LoginActivity" >
</activity>
```

10. Import the `NfcHelper` class to the project.

11. Add the following class members:

```java
public class MainActivity extends Activity implements
    CreateNdefMessageCallback, OnNdefPushCompleteCallback {

    private Context context;
    private ProfilePictureView profilePictureView;
```

```java
private TextView txtUserName;
private TextView txtUserId;

private NfcHelper nfcHelper;
private Handler handler;

private String fbUserId;
...
}
```

12. Override the `onCreate` method and insert the following code:

```java
@Override
protected void onCreate(Bundle savedInstanceState) {
  super.onCreate(savedInstanceState);
  setContentView(R.layout.activity_main);

  context = this;

  profilePictureView = (ProfilePictureView) findViewById(R.
id.profilePicture);
  txtUserName = (TextView) findViewById(R.id.txtUserName);
  txtUserId = (TextView) findViewById(R.id.txtUserId);

  nfcHelper = new NfcHelper(this);

  handler = new Handler() {
    @Override
    public void handleMessage(Message msg) {

      Toast.makeText(getApplicationContext(), "Beam sent!", Toast.
LENGTH_LONG).show();

    }
  };

  facebookLogin();
}
```

13. Implement the `facebookLogin` method with the following code:

```java
void facebookLogin() {
  Session.openActiveSession(this, true, new Session.
StatusCallback() {
```

```java
        @Override
        public void call(Session session, SessionState state,
    Exception exception) {

            if (session.isOpened()) {

            Request.newMeRequest(session, new GraphUserCallback() {

              @Override
              public void onCompleted(GraphUser user, Response response)
        {
                if (user != null) {
                  txtUserId.setText(user.getId());
                txtUserName.setText(user.getName());
                profilePictureView.setProfileId(user.getId());

                fbUserId = user.getId();
                }


              }
            }).executeAsync();

          }


          }
        });
    }
```

14. Implement the following `CreateNdefMessageCallback` interface and the corresponding `createNdefMessage` method in `MainActivity`:

```java
public class MainActivity extends Activity implements
    CreateNdefMessageCallback {
...

@Override
public NdefMessage createNdefMessage(NfcEvent event) {

  try {

    return nfcHelper.createExternalTypeNdefMessage("nfcbookch7exam
ple2", fbUserId.getBytes("UTF-8"));

  } catch (UnsupportedEncodingException e) {
```

```
        Log.e("createNdefMessage", e.getMessage());
    }

    return null;
}
```

15. Implement the following `OnNdefPushCompleteCallback` interface and the corresponding `onNdefPushComplete` method in `MainActivity`:

```
public class MainActivity extends Activity implements
    CreateNdefMessageCallback, OnNdefPushCompleteCallback {

...

    @Override
    public void onNdefPushComplete(NfcEvent event) {
      handler.obtainMessage(1).sendToTarget();
    }

}
```

16. Enable `NdefPush` on `MainActivity` by adding the following lines of code in the `onCreate` method:

```
protected void onCreate(Bundle savedInstanceState) {

    ...

    NfcAdapter nfcAdapter = NfcAdapter.getDefaultAdapter(this);

    nfcAdapter.setNdefPushMessageCallback(this, this);
    nfcAdapter.setOnNdefPushCompleteCallback(this, this);

}
```

17. Implement the `handleIntent` method with the following code:

```
private void handleIntent(Intent intent) {

    if (!nfcHelper.isNfcIntent(intent)) {
      return;
    }

    NdefMessage ndefMessage = nfcHelper.getNdefMessageFromIntent
(intent);
    NdefRecord ndefRecord = nfcHelper.getFirstNdefRecord
(ndefMessage);
```

```java
    String receivedUserId = nfcHelper.getTextFromNdefRecord
(ndefRecord);

    showFriendRequestDialog(receivedUserId);
}
```

18. Override the `onNewIntent` method and insert the following code:

```java
@Override
public void onNewIntent(Intent intent) {
    setIntent(intent);
}
```

19. Implement the `showFriendRequestDialog` method with the following code:

```java
private void showFriendRequestDialog(String userId) {
    Bundle params = new Bundle();
    params.putString("id", userId);

    WebDialog dialog = new WebDialog.Builder(context, Session.
getActiveSession(), "friends", params).setOnCompleteListener(new
WebDialog.OnCompleteListener() {
        @Override
        public void onComplete(Bundle values, FacebookException error)
{

        }
    }).build();

    dialog.show();
}
```

20. Override the `onResume` method and insert the following code:

```java
@Override
public void onResume() {
    super.onResume();

    handleIntent(getIntent());
}
```

21. Override the `onActivityResult` method and insert the following code:

```java
@Override
public void onActivityResult(int requestCode, int resultCode,
Intent data) {
```

```
    super.onActivityResult(requestCode, resultCode, data);
    Session.getActiveSession().onActivityResult(this, requestCode,
resultCode, data);
}
```

22. Run the application on two smartphones and allow the Facebook application to access your account.

23. Once you do this, your Facebook account image, your name, and ID should appear.

24. Tap on one of the devices to send your Facebook ID to the other device.

25. A **Beam sent!** toast should appear in the device that has been touched and a Facebook friend request dialog should appear in the other.

> An alternative way to using the friend request dialog is opening the Facebook profile page. This can be done using the following method:
>
> ```
> private void openFbApp(String userId) {
>     Intent fbIntent = new Intent(Intent.ACTION_VIEW, Uri.
> parse("fb://profile/" + userId));
>
>     PackageManager packageManager = getPackageManager();
>
>     if (packageManager.queryIntentActivities(fbIntent,
> 0).size() == 0) {
>         fbIntent = new Intent(Intent.ACTION_VIEW, Uri.
> parse("https://www.facebook.com/" + userId));
>     }
>
>     startActivity(fbIntent);
> }
> ```

How it works...

This application requires Facebook to be installed because at the application startup, we request the user's Facebook login details, and it uses the current Facebook application session. We also store the current user ID and name. When both devices get close and `NdefMessage` gets pushed, the user ID is sent using a simple message formatted in the `RTD_EXTERNAL_TYPE` pattern, and at the receiving end, the ID is obtained from the NDEF message and a friend request dialog is shown. From that point on, it is the user who decides whether or not to send the friend request. We cannot do that automatically since the Facebook API doesn't allow this.

Inviting a friend to play a game – Part 1

Most of us have certainly played games that involve challenging someone to beat your record or inviting your friend to play against you. These invites are normally made using Facebook, or on e-mail, or even by SMS. In this recipe, we will create a simple application and implement an NFC-invite system that can be used together with the traditional invite methods.

How to do it...

In this application, we will create a simple method to share the player's information through an external-typed NDEF message. This information will be used later to allow Bluetooth pairing. This can be done by performing the following steps:

1. Open Eclipse and create a new Android application project named `NfcBookCh7Example4` and a package named `nfcbook.ch7.example4`.

2. Make sure the `AndroidManifest.xml` file is configured correctly —refer to the *Requesting NFC permissions* recipe in *Chapter 1, Getting Started with NFC*.

3. Set the minimum SDK version to `16` with the following code:

```
<uses-sdk android:minSdkVersion="16" />
```

4. Request Bluetooth permission with the following code:

```
<uses-permission android:name="android.permission.BLUETOOTH" />
```

5. Add the following `intent-filter` to `MainActivity` in the `AndroidManifest` file:

```
<intent-filter>
  <action android:name="android.nfc.action.NDEF_DISCOVERED" />

  <category android:name="android.intent.category.DEFAULT" />

  <data
    andrcid:host="ext"
    andrcid:pathPrefix="/com.packtpub:ch7example4type"
    andrcid:scheme="vnd.android.nfc" />
</intent-filter>
```

6. Replace the content of the `activity_main.xml` file located at `/res/layout` with the following code:

```
<RelativeLayout xmlns:android="http://schemas.android.com/apk/res/
android"
    xmlns:tools="http://schemas.android.com/tools"
    android:layout_width="match_parent"
```

```xml
    android:layout_height="match_parent"
    android:paddingBottom="@dimen/activity_vertical_margin"
    android:paddingLeft="@dimen/activity_horizontal_margin"
    android:paddingRight="@dimen/activity_horizontal_margin"
    android:paddingTop="@dimen/activity_vertical_margin"
    tools:context=".MainActivity" >

    <Button
        android:id="@+id/btInviteNfc"
        android:layout_width="wrap_content"
        android:layout_height="wrap_content"
        android:layout_alignParentBottom="true"
        android:layout_alignParentLeft="true"
        android:layout_alignParentRight="true"
        android:onClick="onBtInviteNfcClick"
        android:text="invite friend over nfc" />

    <TextView
        android:id="@+id/textView1"
        android:layout_width="wrap_content"
        android:layout_height="wrap_content"
        android:layout_alignParentLeft="true"
        android:layout_alignParentTop="true"
        android:text="Opponent:" />

    <TextView
        android:id="@+id/txtOpponentName"
        android:layout_width="wrap_content"
        android:layout_height="wrap_content"
        android:layout_alignBottom="@+id/textView1"
        android:layout_alignParentRight="true"
        android:layout_marginLeft="10dip"
        android:layout_toRightOf="@+id/textView1"
        android:text="" />

    <TextView
        android:id="@+id/textView2"
        android:layout_width="wrap_content"
        android:layout_height="wrap_content"
        android:layout_centerHorizontal="true"
        android:layout_centerVertical="true"
        android:text="your awesome game here."
        android:textAppearance="?android:attr/textAppearanceLarge"
/>

</RelativeLayout>
```

The previous code creates a layout that is identical to the following screenshot:

7. Add a new class named `Player` with the following code:

```java
public class Player implements Serializable {

    private String Name;
    private String Address;

    public String getName() {
        return Name;
    }

    public void setName(String name) {
        Name = name;
    }
```

```java
public String getAddress() {
  return Address;
}


public void setAddress(String address) {
  Address = address;
}
}
```

8. Import the `NfcHelper` class into the project.

9. Add the following class members to `MainActivity`:

```java
private BluetoothAdapter btAdapter;
private NfcHelper nfcHelper;
private Handler handler;
private ProgressDialog waitingDialog;
```

10. Override the `onCreate` method and insert the following code:

```java
@Override
protected void onCreate(Bundle savedInstanceState) {
  super.onCreate(savedInstanceState);
  setContentView(R.layout.activity_main);

  btAdapter = BluetoothAdapter.getDefaultAdapter();

  if (btAdapter == null) {
    Toast.makeText(getApplicationContext(), "Bluetooth not
available", Toast.LENGTH_SHORT).show();

    finish();
    return;
  }

  nfcHelper = new NfcHelper(this);

  handler = new Handler() {
    @Override
    public void handleMessage(Message msg) {

      Toast.makeText(getApplicationContext(), "Beam sent!", Toast.
LENGTH_LONG).show();

    }
  };
}
```

11. Implement the following `CreateNdefMessageCallback` interface and the corresponding `createNdefMessage` method in `MainActivity`:

```java
public class MainActivity extends Activity implements
    CreateNdefMessageCallback {

...

@Override
public NdefMessage createNdefMessage(NfcEvent event) {
  Player player = new Player();

  player.setAddress(btAdapter.getAddress());
  player.setName(btAdapter.getName());

  return nfcHelper.createExternalTypeNdefMessage("ch7example4ty
pe", objectToBytes(player));
}
```

12. Implement the following `OnNdefPushCompleteCallback` interface and the corresponding `onNdefPushComplete` method in `MainActivity`:

```java
public class MainActivity extends Activity implements
    CreateNdefMessageCallback, OnNdefPushCompleteCallback {

...

  @Override
  public void onNdefPushComplete(NfcEvent event) {
    handler.obtainMessage(1).sendToTarget();
  }

}
```

13. Implement the `handleIntent` method with the following code:

```java
private void handleIntent(Intent intent) {

  if (!nfcHelper.isNfcIntent(intent)) {
    return;
  }

  if (waitingDialog != null) {
    waitingDialog.dismiss();
  }

  NdefMessage ndefMessage = nfcHelper.getNdefMessageFromIntent
(intent);
```

```
    NdefRecord ndefRecord = nfcHelper.getFirstNdefRecord
(ndefMessage);

    Player player = (Player) bytesToObject(ndefRecord.getPayload());

    ((TextView) findViewById(R.id.txtOpponentName)).setText(player.
getName());

}
```

14. Override the `onNewIntent` method and insert the following code:

```
@Override
public void onNewIntent(Intent intent) {
  setIntent(intent);
}
```

15. Override the `onResume` method and insert the following code:

```
@Override
public void onResume() {
  super.onResume();

  handleIntent(getIntent());
}
```

16. Implement the `objectToBytes` method with the following code:

```
byte[] objectToBytes(Object obj) {
  ByteArrayOutputStream bos = new ByteArrayOutputStream();
  ObjectOutput out = null;

  try {
    out = new ObjectOutputStream(bos);
    out.writeObject(obj);

    out.close();
    bos.close();

  } catch (Exception e) {
    Log.e("objectToBytes", e.getMessage());
  }

  return bos.toByteArray();
}
```

17. Implement the bytesToObject method:

```
Object bytesToObject(byte[] bytes) {
  Object o = null;
  ByteArrayInputStream bis = new ByteArrayInputStream(bytes);
  ObjectInput in = null;

  try {
    in = new ObjectInputStream(bis);

    o = in.readObject();

    bis.close();
  } catch (Exception e) {
    Log.e("bytesToObject", e.getMessage());
  }
  return o;
}
```

18. Implement the `onBtInviteNfcClick` method with the following code:

```
public void onBtInviteNfcClick(View view) {
  waitingDialog = new ProgressDialog(this);
  waitingDialog.setMessage("Waiting for opponent...");
  waitingDialog.setCancelable(true);

  NfcAdapter nfcAdapter = NfcAdapter.getDefaultAdapter(this);
  nfcAdapter.setNdefPushMessageCallback(this, this);
  nfcAdapter.setOnNdefPushCompleteCallback(this, this);

  waitingDialog.show();
}
```

19. Run the application on two smartphones, tap the **Invite friend over Nfc** button, and bring them close with their backs facing each other.

20. Tap on one of the devices to send the player's details to the other device.

21. A **Beam sent!** toast should appear in the device that was touched, and the player's name should appear in the other device.

How it works...

The player information consists of his device name and address. We make use of the Bluetooth adapter to get this information. The player name corresponds to the device's Bluetooth name and the address corresponds to the Bluetooth's MAC address. This address will be used later to pair both the devices and enable a constant connection for the game.

The `Player` class is serialized in `byte[]` and placed in an external `NdefMessage` type. When the message is pushed to the other device, `byte[]` is deserialized into a `Player` class instance and then we can turn Bluetooth ON and pair the devices. This will be done in the *Inviting a friend to play a game – Part 2* recipe in *Chapter 9, Extending NFC*.

8

Error Handling and Content Validation

In this chapter, we will cover the following topics:

- ► Handling tag-writing errors
- ► Handling tag-reading errors
- ► Testing the tag data for integrity

Introduction

One of the experiences that users probably hate the most is having an application crash while they are using it. Since we don't want our application users to get angry, we are going to take some extra precautions while reading and writing our tags. In this chapter, we will go through some recipes with simple but really helpful tips on how to prevent some unwanted errors.

Handling tag-writing errors

In this recipe, we will modify the `NfcHelper` write methods to throw both custom and native exceptions to allow us to correctly identify what went wrong during the write operation. This will make our applications more bulletproof and user friendly.

Getting ready

The following settings need to be configured for the recipe:

- Make sure you have a working Android development environment. If you don't, ADT Bundle is a good kit to start with (`http://developer.android.com/sdk/index.html`).

- Make sure you have NFC-enabled Android device or a virtual test environment. Refer to the *Testing your app all together* recipe in *Chapter 1*, *Getting Started with NFC*.

- It will be assumed that Eclipse is the development IDE.

How to do it...

In this application, we will be tweaking the `writeNdefMessage` and `formatTag` methods we have used so far in the book. We will use the code files from the *Leaving a (small) note – Part 2* recipe of *Chapter 6*, *Reading Tag Content – Real-life Examples*, to perform the following steps:

1. Open the code files of the *Leaving a (small) note – Part 2* recipe of *Chapter 6*, *Reading Tag Content – Real-life Examples*. Alternatively, we can import the files into a new project named `NfcBookCh8Example1` and a package named `nfcbook.ch8.example1`.

2. Add the following strings to the `res/values/strings.xml` file:

```xml
<string name="toast_error_read_only_tag">Tag is read
  only.</string>
<string name="toast_error_not_ndefformatable">Tag is not
  NdefFormatable.</string>
<string name="toast_error_formatting">Error formatting tag
  as Ndef.</string>
<string name="toast_error_tag_lost">Tag lost or pulled away
  while writing.</string>
<string name="toast_error_no_ndef">NDEF format not
  supported.</string>
<string name="toast_error_no_size">Insufficient tag
  size.</string>
<string name="toast_error_unknown">Unknown error while
  writing tag.</string>
```

3. Create a new package named `nfcbook.ch8.example1.exceptions`.

4. Add a new class named `InsufficientSizeException` to the newly created package named `nfcbook.ch8.example1.exceptions` as follows:

```java
public class InsufficientSizeException extends Exception {

  private int requiredTagSize;
  private int availableTagSize;

  public InsufficientSizeException(int required, int
    available){

  }

  @Override
  public String getMessage() {
    String message = "Insufficient tag size. required:%s,
      available: %s";

    return String.format(message, requiredTagSize,
      availableTagSize);
  }
}
```

5. Add a new class named `ReadOnlyTagException` to the `nfcbook.ch8.example1.exceptions` package as follows:

```java
public class ReadOnlyTagException extends Exception {

  public ReadOnlyTagException(){
    super("Tag is read only.");
  }

}
```

6. Add a new class named `NdefFormatException` to the `nfcbook.ch8.example1.exceptions` package:

```java
public class NdefFormatException extends Exception {

  public NdefFormatException() {
    super("Error formatting tag as Ndef");
  }

}
```

7. Open the `NfcHelper` class and replace the `formatTag` method with the following code:

```java
private void formatTag(Tag tag, NdefMessage ndefMessage)
  throws IOException, FormatException, NdefFormatException
    {

  NdefFormatable ndefFormat = NdefFormatable.get(tag);

  if (ndefFormat == null) {
    throw new NdefFormatException();
  }


  ndefFormat.connect();
  ndefFormat.format(ndefMessage);
  ndefFormat.close();
}
```

8. Replace `writeNdefMessage` of the `NdefHelper` class with the following code:

```java
private void writeNdefMessage(Tag tag, NdefMessage
  ndefMessage) throws IOException, FormatException,
    ReadOnlyTagException, InsufficientSizeException,
      NdefFormatException {

  Ndef ndef = Ndef.get(tag);

  if (ndef == null) {
    formatTag(tag, ndefMessage);
  } else {

    ndef.connect();

    int maxSize = ndef.getMaxSize();
    int messageSize = ndefMessage.toByteArray().length;

    if (!ndef.isWritable()) {

      throw new ReadOnlyTagException();

    } else if (maxSize < messageSize) {

      throw new InsufficientSizeException(messageSize,
        maxSize);
```

```
    } else {

      ndef.writeNdefMessage(ndefMessage);
      ndef.close();

    }

  }
}
```

9. Open `MainActivity` and replace the `onNewIntent` method with the following code:

```
@Override
protected void onNewIntent(Intent intent) {

  if (nfcHelper.isNfcIntent(intent)) {
    if (isWritingTag) {

      String text = txtNote.getText().toString();

      NdefMessage ndefMsg =
        nfcHelper.createTextNdefMessage(text);

      try {

        nfcHelper.writeNdefMessage(intent, ndefMsg);

        Toast.makeText(this,
          R.string.toast_write_successful,
            Toast.LENGTH_LONG).show();

      } catch (TagLostException e) {

        Toast.makeText(this, R.string.toast_error_tag_lost,
          Toast.LENGTH_LONG).show();

      } catch (IOException e) {

        Toast.makeText(this,
          R.string.toast_error_formatting,
            Toast.LENGTH_LONG).show();

      } catch (FormatException e) {
```

```java
      Toast.makeText(this,
        R.string.toast_error_formatting,
          Toast.LENGTH_LONG).show();

    } catch (ReadOnlyTagException e) {

      Toast.makeText(this,
        R.string.toast_error_read_only_tag,
          Toast.LENGTH_LONG).show();

    } catch (InsufficientSizeException e) {

      Toast.makeText(this, e.getMessage(),
        Toast.LENGTH_LONG).show();

    } catch (NdefFormatException e) {

      Toast.makeText(this,
        R.string.toast_error_not_ndefformatable,
          Toast.LENGTH_LONG).show();

    } catch (Exception e) {

      Toast.makeText(this, R.string.toast_error_unknown,
        Toast.LENGTH_LONG).show();

    }

    isWritingTag = false;
    writingProgressDialog.dismiss();

  } else {
    NdefMessage ndefMessage =
      nfcHelper.getNdefMessageFromIntent(intent);

    if (ndefMessage != null) {

      NdefRecord ndefRecord =
        nfcHelper.getFirstNdefRecord(ndefMessage);

      if (ndefRecord != null) {

        String text =
          nfcHelper.getTextFromNdefRecord(ndefRecord);
```

```
            txtNote.setText(text);

        } else {
          Log.i("onNewIntent", "No NdefRecord found.");
        }

      } else {
        Log.i("onNewIntent", "No NdefMessage found.");
      }

    }
  }
}
```

10. Run the application and try to get the different error messages using the following methods:

   ❑ Write long messages to a tag

   ❑ Move away the smartphone quickly while writing a tag

   ❑ Try to write content to a locked tag

How it works...

We created some custom exceptions that we use together with the ones already thrown by the Android API so that we can know more accurately what happened while writing, as described in the following list:

- `TagLostException`: This exception is thrown by the Android API when the connection to the tag is lost. Usually, this occurs when the user moves away the device before the operation is complete.

- `ReadOnlyTagException`: This exception is thrown when we are trying to write on a locked tag.

- `InsufficientSizeException`: This exception is thrown when we are trying to write a long message whose size is than the available size tag.

- `FormatException`: This exception is thrown by the Android API when the tag type is not compatible with the one we are trying to format it to.

- `NdefFormatException`: This exception is thrown when the tag cannot be formatted as `Ndef`.

- `IOException`: This exception is thrown by the Android API when a problem has occurred during the communication with the tag.

This way, we can display different messages to the user, informing him or her what exactly happened.

Handling tag-reading errors

In this recipe, we will implement generic validation methods to identify the tag format. This way, we can implement different payload handling mechanisms for the content that our application knows to handle, preventing unwanted exceptions.

Getting ready

We will be using the project from the previous recipe, so make sure you have gone through it before starting this one.

How to do it...

In this application, we will be adding some methods to your `NfcHelper` class to facilitate the identification of the tag content. To do this, perform the following steps:

1. Open the project files from the *Handling tag-writing errors* recipe.

2. Implement the `isTextRecord` method in the `NfcHelper` class with the following code:

    ```java
    public boolean isTextRecord(NdefRecord record) {

      if (record == null) {
        return false;
      }

      return isNdefRecordOfTnfAndRdt(record,
        NdefRecord.TNF_WELL_KNOWN, NdefRecord.RTD_TEXT);
    }
    ```

3. Implement the `isUrlRecord` method in the `NfcHelper` class:

    ```java
    public boolean isUriRecord(NdefRecord record) {

      if (record == null) {
        return false;
      }

      return isNdefRecordOfTnfAndRdt(record,
        NdefRecord.TNF_WELL_KNOWN, NdefRecord.RTD_URI);
    }
    ```

4. Implement the `isMimeRecord` method in the `NfcHelper` class:

```java
public boolean isMimeRecord(NdefRecord record, String
  mimeType) {

    if (record == null || mimeType == null) {
      return false;
    }

    byte[] mimeBytes =
      mimeType.getBytes(Charset.forName("US-ASCII"));

    return isNdefRecordOfTnfAndRdt(record,
      NdefRecord.TNF_MIME_MEDIA, mimeBytes);
}
```

5. Implement the isExternalTypeRecord method in the NfcHelper class:

```java
public boolean isExternalTypeRecord(NdefRecord record,
  String domain, String type) {

    if (record == null || domain == null || type == null) {
      return false;
    }

    byte[] externalTypeBytes = String.format("%s:%s",
      domain, type).getBytes(Charset.forName("US-ASCII"));

    return isNdefRecordOfTnfAndRdt(record,
      NdefRecord.TNF_EXTERNAL_TYPE, externalTypeBytes);
}
```

6. Add the `NdefMessage` validation in the `onNewIntent` method:

```java
@Override
protected void onNewIntent(Intent intent) {

    if (nfcHelper.isNfcIntent(intent)) {
      if (isWritingTag) {
        ...
      } else {
        NdefMessage ndefMessage =
          nfcHelper.getNdefMessageFromIntent(intent);

        if (ndefMessage != null) {
```

```java
NdefRecord ndefRecord =
  nfcHelper.getFirstNdefRecord(ndefMessage);

if (nfcHelper.isTextRecord(ndefRecord)) {

  Toast.makeText(this, "text formated tag",
    Toast.LENGTH_LONG).show();

  String text =
    nfcHelper.getTextFromNdefRecord(ndefRecord);

  txtNote.setText(text);

} else if (nfcHelper.isUriRecord(ndefRecord)) {

  Toast.makeText(this, "uri formated tag",
    Toast.LENGTH_LONG).show();
  startActivity(intent);

} else if (nfcHelper.isMimeRecord(ndefRecord,
  "application/mymime")) {

  Toast.makeText(this, "mimed formated tag",
    Toast.LENGTH_LONG).show();
  startActivity(intent);

} else if
  (nfcHelper.isExternalTypeRecord(ndefRecord,
    "packtpub.com", "myexternaltype")) {

  Toast.makeText(this, "this is an external type
    formated tag", Toast.LENGTH_LONG).show();
  startActivity(intent);

} else {

  Toast.makeText(this, "unknown tag format",
    Toast.LENGTH_LONG).show();

}

} else {
  Log.i("onNewIntent", "No NdefMessage found.");
}
```

```
        }
      }

    }
```

7. Save different tags with different content types.

8. Tap the different content tag, which is formatted, on your smartphone. A toast that indicates whether or not the type is recognized should appear.

How it works...

When we are developing applications that need to be capable of interpreting different tag content types, one of the outcomes we don't want is to handle the payload the wrong way. The implemented `isTextRecord`, `isUriRecord`, `isMimeRecord`, and `isExternalTypeRecord` methods allow us to implement specific instructions for each of the tag formats only if we know how to handle it.

Testing the tag data for integrity

In this recipe, we will create a simple project to demonstrate a simple way to test for data integrity using and MD5 hash.

Getting ready

We will be using the project from the previous recipe, so make sure you have gone through it.

How to do it...

In this application, we will be adding an additional `NdefRecord` instance into our `NdefMessage`, which contains the MD5 hash of the main message that will allow us to test for data integrity. Perform the following steps:

1. Open the project files from the *Handling tag-reading errors* recipe.

2. Implement the `getMd5Hash` method in the `NfcHelper` class:

```java
private byte[] getMd5Hash(byte[] message) {

    byte[] salt =
      "nfcbook.ch8.example3".getBytes(Charset.forName("US-
        ASCII"));

    try {
```

```java
        MessageDigest md = MessageDigest.getInstance("MD5");

        ByteArrayOutputStream stream = new
          ByteArrayOutputStream();

        stream.write(message);
        stream.write(salt);

        return md.digest(stream.toByteArray());

      } catch (Exception e) {
        Log.e("getMd5Hash", e.getMessage());
      }

      return null;
    }
```

3. Implement the `CreateHashRecord` method in the `NfcHelper` class:

```java
    public NdefRecord createHashRecord(byte[] message) {

        return NdefRecord.createExternal("com.packtpub",
          "hash", getMd5Hash(message));

    }
```

4. Modify the `createTextNdefMessage` method and add `NdefRecord` that contains the content MD5 hash as part of `NdefMessage`:

```java
    public NdefMessage createTextNdefMessage(String text) {

        NdefRecord record = createTextRecord(text);
        NdefRecord hashRecord =
          createHashRecord(record.toByteArray());

        return new NdefMessage(new NdefRecord[] { record,
          hashRecord });
    }
```

5. Implement the `checkNdefDataIntegrity` method in the `NfcHelper` class:

```java
    public boolean checkNdefDataIntegrity(NdefMessage
      ndefMessage) throws Exception {

        NdefRecord[] records = ndefMessage.getRecords();
```

```java
if (records.length < 2) {
  throw new Exception("Invalid NdefRecord count");
}

if (!isExternalTypeRecord(records[1], "com.packtpub",
  "controlhash")) {
  throw new Exception("NdefRecord[1] is not a valid
    hash record");
}

byte[] payloadHash =
  getMd5Hash(records[0].toByteArray());
byte[] messageHash = records[1].getPayload();

return Arrays.equals(payloadHash, messageHash);
}
```

6. Add the `NdefMessage` validation in the `onNewIntent` method:

```java
@Override
protected void onNewIntent(Intent intent) {

  if (nfcHelper.isNfcIntent(intent)) {
    if (isWritingTag) {

      ...

    } else {
      NdefMessage ndefMessage =
        nfcHelper.getNdefMessageFromIntent(intent);

      if (ndefMessage != null) {

        try {

          if (nfcHelper.checkNdefDataIntegrity
            (ndefMessage)) {
            Toast.makeText(this, "Data hash ok!",
              Toast.LENGTH_LONG).show();
          } else {
            Toast.makeText(this, "Data hash not ok!",
              Toast.LENGTH_LONG).show();
          }
```

```
        } catch (Exception e) {
          Toast.makeText(this, e.getMessage(),
            Toast.LENGTH_LONG).show();
        }

      } else {
        Log.i("onNewIntent", "No NdefMessage found.");
      }

    }
  }

}
```

7. Run the application and write a message to a tag.

8. Read the tag with your smartphone and a **Data hash ok!** toast should appear.

How it works...

As you already know, `NdefMessage` is composed of several `NdefRecords`, and each of those `NdefRecords` can hold different types of content. In this recipe, we make use of the fact that we can add several records to add one containing the MD5 message digest of the main record. For additional security, we also add a `Salt` value (`http://en.wikipedia.org/wiki/Salt_(cryptography)`) to the message before generating the MD5 hash. While reading the tag content, we get both records; regenerate the MD5 digest and compare it with the one from the tag. If they both match, we know that the content of the main record wasn't changed since it was written to the tag. The NFC protocol already includes checksums that tries to guarantee us that the data transferred during reading and writing operations is not changed. With this validation, we try to guarantee that the tag was indeed written by our application, and that the main record did not suffer any malicious changes in the content.

9

Extending NFC

In this chapter, we will cover the following topics:

- ▶ Turning other adapters on/off
- ▶ Configuring a Wi-Fi network
- ▶ Starting a Wi-Fi hotspot
- ▶ Inviting a friend to play a game – Part 2
- ▶ Controlling hotel room access with Arduino and NFC – Part 1
- ▶ Controlling hotel room access with Arduino and NFC – Part 2

Introduction

NFC communication by itself doesn't provide us with many features due to its small data transfer characteristics. For instance, we can only exchange small data packages between devices, and tag sizes are also (very) small. In this chapter, we will see how NFC can be used to enable adapters such as Bluetooth so that we can take advantage of NFC characteristics while still being able to create more complex apps.

Turning other adapters on/off

In this recipe, we will create a basic application that writes enable/disable actions to a tag and enables/disables the chosen adapter when the tag is detected.

Getting ready

In order to create a basic application that will turn the adapters on/off, make sure that you take care of the following elements:

- Make sure you have a working Android development environment. If you don't, ADT Bundle is a good start. It is available at `http://developer.android.com/sdk/index.html`.

- Also, you should have an NFC-enabled Android device or a virtual test environment. Refer to the *Testing your app all together* recipe in *Chapter 1, Getting Started with NFC*.

- We assume that Eclipse is your development IDE and that you are familiar with writing external-type `NdefRecords`. Refer to the *Working with external types* recipe in *Chapter 3, Writing Tag Content*.

How to do it...

We will write an `Integer` value to a tag. This value represents an action to enable/disable Wi-Fi, network, GPS, and Bluetooth. When the tag is read, the application will perform the saved action:

1. Open Eclipse and create a new Android application project named `NfcBookCh9Example1` and package named `nfcbook.ch9.example1`.

2. Make sure the `AndroidManifest.xml` file is correctly configured. Refer to the *Requesting NFC permissions* recipe in *Chapter 1, Getting Started with NFC*.

3. Request for permission to change the adapter's state by adding the following lines of code to `AndroidManifest.xml`:

```
<uses-permission
  android:name="android.permission.BLUETOOTH" />
<uses-permission
  android:name="android.permission.ACCESS_WIFI_STATE" />
<uses-permission
  android:name="android.permission.CHANGE_WIFI_STATE" />
<uses-permission
  android:name="android.permission.CHANGE_NETWORK_STATE" />
<uses-permission
  android:name="android.permission.ACCESS_FINE_LOCATION" />
<uses-permission
  android:name="android.permission.BLUETOOTH_ADMIN" />
```

4. Add `intent-filter` to `MainActivity` in the `AndroidManifest` file:

```
<intent-filter>
  <action android:name="android.nfc.action.
    NDEF_DISCOVERED" />
```

```xml
<category android:name="android.intent.category.
  DEFAULT" />

<data
  android:host="ext"
  android:pathPrefix="/com.packtpub:ch9example1type"
  android:scheme="vnd.android.nfc" />

</intent-filter>
```

5. Add the following `string` to the `res/values/strings.xml` file:

```xml
<string name="button_enable_wifi">enable Wifi</string>
<string name="button_disable_wifi">disable Wifi</string>
<string name="button_enable_network">enable
  Network</string>
<string name="button_disable_network">disable
  Network</string>
<string name="button_enable_gps">enable Gps</string>
<string name="button_disable_gps">disable Gps</string>
<string name="dialog_waiting_tag">Waiting tag...</string>
<string name="button_enable_bluetooth">enable
  Bluetooth</string>
<string name="button_disable_bluetooth">disable
  Bluetooth</string>
<string name="label_choose_action">Choose an action to
  write</string>
```

6. Replace the content in the `activity_main.xml` file located at `/res/layout` with the following:

```xml
<ScrollView xmlns:android=
  "http://schemas.android.com/apk/res/android"
    xmlns:tools="http://schemas.android.com/tools"
    android:layout_width="match_parent"
    android:layout_height="match_parent"
    android:paddingBottom="@dimen/activity_vertical_margin"
    android:paddingLeft="@dimen/activity_horizontal_margin"
    android:paddingRight=
      "@dimen/activity_horizontal_margin"
    android:paddingTop="@dimen/activity_vertical_margin"
    tools:context=".MainActivity" >

    <LinearLayout
        android:layout_width="match_parent"
```

```xml
    android:layout_height="wrap_content"
    android:orientation="vertical" >

<TextView
    android:id="@+id/textView1"
    android:layout_width="match_parent"
    android:layout_height="wrap_content"
    android:text="@string/label_choose_action"
    android:textAppearance=
      "?android:attr/textAppearanceMedium"
    android:layout_marginBottom="10dip"/>

<Button
    android:id="@+id/btEnableWifi"
    android:layout_width="match_parent"
    android:layout_height="wrap_content"
    android:onClick="onBtEnableWifiClick"
    android:text="@string/button_enable_wifi" />

<Button
    android:id="@+id/btDisableWifi"
    android:layout_width="match_parent"
    android:layout_height="wrap_content"
    android:onClick="onBtDisableWifiClick"
    android:text="@string/button_disable_wifi" />

<Button
    android:id="@+id/btEnableBluetooth"
    android:layout_width="match_parent"
    android:layout_height="wrap_content"
    android:onClick="onBtEnableBluetooth"
    android:text=
      "@string/button_enable_bluetooth" />

<Button
    android:id="@+id/btDisableBluetooth"
    android:layout_width="match_parent"
    android:layout_height="wrap_content"
    android:onClick="onBtDisableBluetooth"
    android:text=
      "@string/button_disable_bluetooth" />

<Button
    android:id="@+id/btEnableNetwork"
    android:layout_width="match_parent"
    android:layout_height="wrap_content"
    android:onClick="onBtEnableNetwork"
    android:text=
      "@string/button_enable_network" />
```

```
<Button
    android:id="@+id/btDisableNetwork"
    android:layout_width="match_parent"
    android:layout_height="wrap_content"
    android:onClick="onBtDisableNetwork"
    android:text=
       "@string/button_disable_network" />

<Button
    android:id="@+id/btEnableGps"
    android:layout_width="match_parent"
    android:layout_height="wrap_content"
    android:onClick="onBtEnableGps"
    android:text=
       "@string/button_enable_gps" />

<Button
    android:id="@+id/btDisableGps"
    android:layout_width="match_parent"
    android:layout_height="wrap_content"
    android:onClick="onBtDisableGps"
    android:text="@string/button_disable_gps" />
    </LinearLayout>

</ScrollView>
```

7. This creates a layout identical to that shown in the following screenshot:

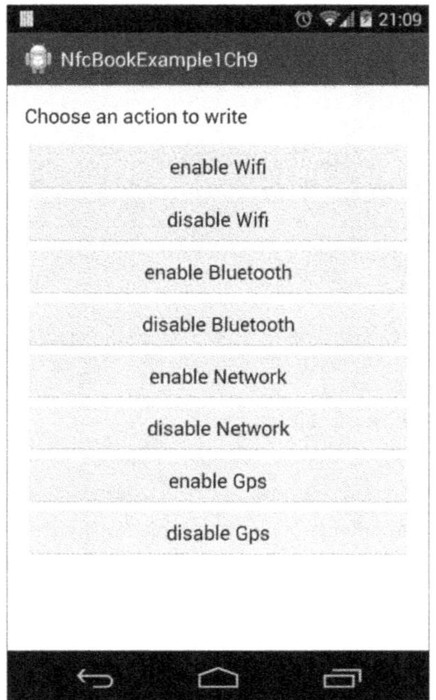

Import the `NfcHelper.java` class into the project and enable the foreground dispatch system by overriding the `onResume` and `onPause` methods:

```
@Override
protected void onResume() {
  super.onResume();

  if (nfcHelper.isNfcEnabledDevice()) {
    nfcHelper.enableForegroundDispatch();
  }
}

@Override
protected void onPause() {
  super.onPause();

  if (nfcHelper.isNfcEnabledDevice()) {
    nfcHelper.disableForegroundDispatch();
  }
}
```

8. Create a new class file named `AdapterHelper` and implement constructor:

```
public AdapterHelper(Context context) {

  this.context = context;

  wifiManager = (WifiManager)
    context.getSystemService(Context.WIFI_SERVICE);

  dataManager = (ConnectivityManager)
    context.getSystemService(Context.CONNECTIVITY_SERVICE);

  locationManager = (LocationManager)
    context.getSystemService(Context.LOCATION_SERVICE);

  bluetoothAdapter = BluetoothAdapter.getDefaultAdapter();
}
```

9. Add the following class members to the `AdapterHelper` class:

```
private Context context;
private WifiManager wifiManager;
private ConnectivityManager dataManager;
private LocationManager locationManager;
private BluetoothAdapter bluetoothAdapter;
```

10. Add `enum` to the `AdapterHelper` class:

```java
public enum AdapterAction {
  ENABLE_WIFI,
  DISABLE_WIFI,
  ENABLE_NETWORK,
  DISABLE_NETWORK,
  ENABLE_GPS,
  DISABLE_GPS,
  ENABLE_BLUETOOTH,
  DISABLE_BLUETOOTH
}
```

11. Implement the methods to change the Wi-Fi states:

```java
public void enableWifi() {

  if (!wifiManager.isWifiEnabled()) {
    wifiManager.setWifiEnabled(true);
  }

}

public void disableWifi() {

  if (!wifiManager.isWifiEnabled()) {
    wifiManager.setWifiEnabled(false);
  }

}
```

12. Implement the methods to change the network states:

```java
public void enableNetwork() {

  try {

    Method dataMtd = ConnectivityManager.class.
      getDeclaredMethod("setMobileDataEnabled", boolean.class);

    dataMtd.setAccessible(true);
    dataMtd.invoke(dataManager, true);

  } catch (Exception e) {
    Log.e("enableNetwork", e.getMessage(), e);
  }
}

public void disableNetwork() {

  try {
```

```java
    Method dataMtd = ConnectivityManager.class.
      getDeclaredMethod("setMobileDataEnabled", boolean.class);

    dataMtd.setAccessible(true);
    dataMtd.invoke(dataManager, false);

  } catch (Exception e) {
    Log.e("disableNetwork", e.getMessage(), e);
  }

}
```

13. Implement the methods to change the Bluetooth states:

```java
public void enableBluetooth() {
  if (bluetoothAdapter != null && !bluetoothAdapter.isEnabled()) {
    bluetoothAdapter.enable();
  }
}

public void disableBluetooth() {
  if (bluetoothAdapter != null && bluetoothAdapter.isEnabled()) {
    bluetoothAdapter.disable();
  }
}
```

14. Implement the methods to change the GPS states:

```java
public void enableGps() {

  if (!locationManager.isProviderEnabled
    (LocationManager.GPS_PROVIDER)) {
    Intent intent = new Intent(android.provider.
      Settings.ACTION_LOCATION_SOURCE_SETTINGS);
    intent.setFlags(Intent.FLAG_ACTIVITY_NEW_TASK);

    context.startActivity(intent);
  }

}

public void disableGps() {

  if (locationManager.isProviderEnabled
    (LocationManager.GPS_PROVIDER)) {
    Intent intent = new Intent(android.provider.
      Settings.ACTION_LOCATION_SOURCE_SETTINGS);
    intent.setFlags(Intent.FLAG_ACTIVITY_NEW_TASK);

    context.startActivity(intent);
  }

}
```

15. Add the following class members to `MainActivity`:

```
private NfcHelper nfcHelper;
private AdapterHelper adapterHelper;
private ProgressDialog waitingDialog;
private AdapterAction actionToWrite = null;
```

16. Initialize the `nfcHelper` and `adapterHelper` fields:

```
@Override
protected void onCreate(Bundle savedInstanceState) {

    ...
  nfcHelper = new NfcHelper(this);
  adapterHelper = new AdapterHelper(this);
}
```

17. Implement the `handleIntent` method:

```
private void handleIntent(Intent intent) {

  if (!nfcHelper.isNfcIntent(intent)) {
    return;
  }

  if (waitingDialog != null && actionToWrite != null) {

    byte[] data = new byte[] { (byte)
      actionToWrite.ordinal() };

    NdefMessage ndefMessage = nfcHelper.
      createExternalTypeNdefMessage("ch9example1type",
        data);

    nfcHelper.writeNdefMessage(intent, ndefMessage);

    waitingDialog.dismiss();

    waitingDialog = null;
    actionToWrite = null;

  } else {

    NdefMessage ndefMessage =
      nfcHelper.getNdefMessageFromIntent(intent);
    NdefRecord ndefRecord = nfcHelper.
      getFirstNdefRecord(ndefMessage);

    int ordinal = ndefRecord.getPayload()[0];
    AdapterAction action = AdapterAction.values()[ordinal];
```

```
    handleAction(action);

  }
}
```

18. Implement the `writeAction` method:

```
private void writeAction(AdapterAction action) {

  waitingDialog = new ProgressDialog(this);
  waitingDialog.setMessage(getString(R.string.dialog_waiting_
tag));
  waitingDialog.setCancelable(true);

  actionToWrite = action;

  waitingDialog.show();
}
```

19. Implement the `handleAction` method:

```
private void handleAction(AdapterAction action) {

  switch (action) {
  case ENABLE_WIFI:
    adapterHelper.enableWifi();
    break;
  case DISABLE_WIFI:
    adapterHelper.disableWifi();
    break;
  case ENABLE_NETWORK:
    adapterHelper.enableNetwork();
    break;
  case DISABLE_NETWORK:
    adapterHelper.disableNetwork();
    break;
  case ENABLE_BLUETOOTH:
    adapterHelper.enableBluetooth();
    break;
  case DISABLE_BLUETOOTH:
    adapterHelper.disableBluetooth();
    break;
  case ENABLE_GPS:
    adapterHelper.enableGps();
    break;
  case DISABLE_GPS:
    adapterHelper.disableGps();
    break;
```

```
  }

}
```

20. Implement the button click event listeners:

```
public void onBtEnableWifiClick(View view) {
  writeAction(AdapterAction.ENABLE_WIFI);
}

public void onBtDisableWifiClick(View view) {
  writeAction(AdapterAction.DISABLE_WIFI);
}

public void onBtEnableNetwork(View view) {
  writeAction(AdapterAction.ENABLE_NETWORK);
}

public void onBtDisableNetwork(View view) {
  writeAction(AdapterAction.DISABLE_NETWORK);
}

public void onBtEnableGps(View view) {
  writeAction(AdapterAction.ENABLE_GPS);
}

public void onBtDisableGps(View view) {
  writeAction(AdapterAction.DISABLE_GPS);
}

public void onBtEnableBluetooth(View view) {
  writeAction(AdapterAction.ENABLE_BLUETOOTH);
}

public void onBtDisableBluetooth(View view) {
  writeAction(AdapterAction.DISABLE_BLUETOOTH);
}
```

21. Call the `handleIntent` method in the `onResume` activity method:

```
@Override
protected void onResume() {
  ...

  handleIntent(getIntent());
}
```

22. Override the `onNewIntent` method:

```java
@Override
public void onNewIntent(Intent intent) {
    setIntent(intent);
}
```

23. Run the application and choose an action to write to the tag.

24. Tap the tag on your phone or simulate a tap in the NFC simulator to write the tag.

25. Tap again on the written tag. The action chosen should be performed, that is, Wi-Fi, Bluetooth, network, or GPS will be enabled/disabled.

How it works...

The `AdapterAction` enumeration contains all the actions known by the application, and each `Button` in the layout writes an `Integer` representation of each action to the tag. When using a smartphone, if we tap on a written tag again, we get `Integer` and convert it back to its `AdapterAction` representation. After that, the `handleAction` method is called and the action is executed using `AdapterHelper`, which contains all the logic related to adapter manipulation.

The objective of this recipe is to demonstrate how we write and read known content from an NFC tag and then enable other adapters that our app may need to function.

A good example of this logic being used is when we place a sticker tag in our smartphone car support to automatically enable the GPS and start the maps application.

Configuring a Wi-Fi network

I'm sure you've experienced friends asking you for your Wi-Fi password when they come over, and I bet that most times the answer is "Don't remember," "I'm not sure," or "Let me check the router sticker." In this recipe, we will learn how to create an application to write a simple Wi-Fi network configuration to an NFC tag that allows us to stick it somewhere around the house.

How to do it...

We will store three Wi-Fi network fields, the SSID, the security type, and the password in the tag. When we read it, we will add the network to our device and enable the Wi-Fi adapter:

1. Open Eclipse and create a new Android application project named `NfcBookCh9Example2` and package named `nfcbook.ch9.example2`.

2. Make sure the `AndroidManifest.xml` file is correctly configured. Refer to the *Requesting NFC permissions* recipe in *Chapter 1, Getting Started with NFC*.

3. Request for permission to change the Wi-Fi adapter state by adding the following lines of code to `AndroidManifest.xml`:

```
<uses-permission android:name=
  "android.permission.ACCESS_WIFI_STATE" />
<uses-permission android:name=
  "android.permission.CHANGE_WIFI_STATE" />
```

4. Add the following `intent-filter` to `MainActivity` in the `AndroidManifest` file:

```
<intent-filter>
  <action android:name="android.nfc.action.NDEF_DISCOVERED"
    />

  <category android:name="android.intent.category.DEFAULT"
    />

  <data
    android:host="ext"
    android:pathPrefix="/com.packtpub:ch9example2type"
    android:scheme="vnd.android.nfc" />
</intent-filter>
```

5. Add the following `string` to the `res/values/strings.xml` file:

```
<string name="label_ssid">SSID</string>
<string name="label_security">Security</string>
<string name="label_password">Password</string>
<string name="dialog_waiting_tag">Waiting tag...</string>
<string name="toast_write_success">Tag written</string>
<string name="toast_write_fail">Failed to write tag</string>
<string name="button_write">Write configs</string>
<string name="button_write_as_text">Write configs (as plain
text)</string>

<string-array name="network_sec_types">
  <item>None</item>
  <item>WEP</item>
  <item>WPA PSK</item>
</string-array>
```

6. Replace the content of the `activity_main.xml` file located at `/res/layout` with the following:

```xml
<RelativeLayout xmlns:android=
  "http://schemas.android.com/apk/res/android"
    xmlns:tools="http://schemas.android.com/tools"
    android:layout_width="match_parent"
    android:layout_height="fill_parent"
    android:paddingBottom="@dimen/activity_vertical_margin"
    android:paddingLeft="@dimen/activity_horizontal_margin"
    android:paddingRight=
      "@dimen/activity_horizontal_margin"
    android:paddingTop="@dimen/activity_vertical_margin"
    tools:context=".MainActivity" >

    <TextView
        android:id="@+id/textView1"
        android:layout_width="wrap_content"
        android:layout_height="wrap_content"
        android:layout_alignParentLeft="true"
        android:layout_alignParentRight="true"
        android:text="@string/label_ssid"
        android:textAppearance=
          "?android:attr/textAppearanceSmall" />

    <EditText
        android:id="@+id/txtSSID"
        android:layout_width="match_parent"
        android:layout_height="wrap_content"
        android:layout_alignParentLeft="true"
        android:layout_alignParentRight="true"
        android:layout_below="@+id/textView1"
        android:ems="10" />

    <TextView
        android:id="@+id/textView2"
        android:layout_width="wrap_content"
        android:layout_height="wrap_content"
        android:layout_alignParentLeft="true"
        android:layout_alignParentRight="true"
        android:layout_below="@+id/txtSSID"
        android:layout_marginTop="20dip"
        android:text="@string/label_security"
        android:textAppearance=
          "?android:attr/textAppearanceSmall" />
```

```xml
<Spinner
    android:id="@+id/dropSecTypes"
    android:layout_width="match_parent"
    android:layout_height="wrap_content"
    android:layout_alignParentLeft="true"
    android:layout_alignParentRight="true"
    android:layout_below="@+id/textView2"
    android:entries="@array/network_sec_types" />

<TextView
    android:id="@+id/textView3"
    android:layout_width="wrap_content"
    android:layout_height="wrap_content"
    android:layout_alignParentLeft="true"
    android:layout_alignParentRight="true"
    android:layout_below="@+id/dropSecTypes"
    android:layout_marginTop="20dip"
    android:text="@string/label_password"
    android:textAppearance=
        "?android:attr/textAppearanceSmall" />

<EditText
    android:id="@+id/txtPassword"
    android:layout_width="match_parent"
    android:layout_height="wrap_content"
    android:layout_alignParentLeft="true"
    android:layout_alignParentRight="true"
    android:layout_below="@+id/textView3"
    android:ems="10"
    android:inputType="textPassword" >

    <requestFocus />
</EditText>

<Button
    android:id="@+id/btSaveAsTex"
    android:layout_width="match_parent"
    android:layout_height="wrap_content"
    android:layout_alignParentBottom="true"
    android:layout_alignParentLeft="true"
    android:layout_alignParentRight="true"
    android:onClick="onBtSaveAsTextClick"
    android:text="@string/button_write_as_text" />
```

```
<Button
    android:id="@+id/btSave"
    android:layout_width="match_parent"
    android:layout_height="wrap_content"
    android:layout_above="@+id/btSaveAsTex"
    android:layout_alignParentLeft="true"
    android:layout_alignParentRight="true"
    android:onClick="onBtSaveClick"
    android:text="@string/button_write" />

</RelativeLayout>
```

7. This creates a layout identical to that in the following screenshot:

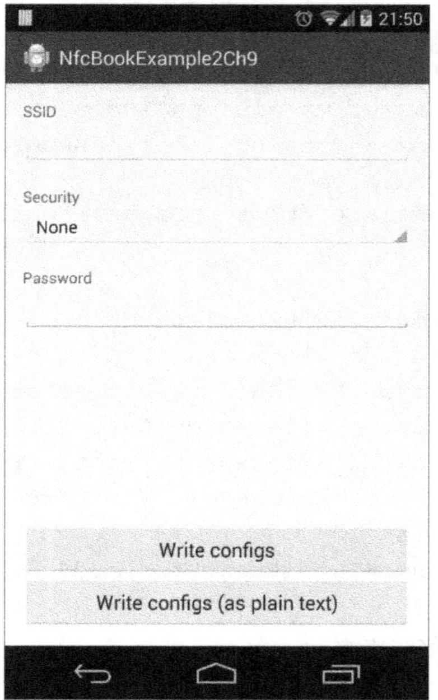

8. Create a new class file named `WifiNetwork` and implement the following `ctors`:

```
public WifiNetwork() {
}

public WifiNetwork(String network) {

  String[] networkParts = network.split("\\|\\:\\|");

  if (networkParts.length != 3) {
    return;
```

```
    }

    ssid = networkParts[0];
    security = networkParts[1];
    password = networkParts[2];
}
```

9. Add the following class members to the `WifiNetwork` class and the corresponding getters and setters:

```java
private String ssid;
private String security;
private String password;

public String getSsid() {
  return ssid;
}

public void setSsid(String ssid) {
  this.ssid = ssid;
}

public String getSecurity() {
  return security;
}

public void setSecurity(String security) {
  this.security = security;
}

public String getPassword() {
  return password;
}

public void setPassword(String password) {
  this.password = password;
}
```

10. Implement the `getWifiConfiguration` method:

```java
public WifiConfiguration getWifiConfiguration() {

    WifiConfiguration wifiConfiguration = new
      WifiConfiguration();

    wifiConfiguration.SSID = "\"" + ssid + "\"";

    if (security.equals("WPE")) {
```

```java
  wifiConfiguration.wepKeys[0] = "\"" + password + "\"";
  wifiConfiguration.wepTxKeyIndex = 0;
wifiConfiguration.allowedKeyManagement.
  set(WifiConfiguration.KeyMgmt.NONE);
wifiConfiguration.allowedGroupCiphers.set
  (WifiConfiguration.GroupCipher.WEP40);

} else if (security.equals("WPA")) {

  wifiConfiguration.preSharedKey
    = "\"" + password + "\"";
wifiConfiguration.allowedKeyManagement.set
  (WifiConfiguration.KeyMgmt.WPA_PSK);
wifiConfiguration.allowedProtocols.set
  (WifiConfiguration.Protocol.WPA);

} else {

wifiConfiguration.allowedKeyManagement.set
  (WifiConfiguration.KeyMgmt.NONE);

}

return wifiConfiguration;
}
```

11. Override the `toString` method:

```java
@Override
public String toString() {
  return String.format("%s|:|%s|:|%s", ssid, security,
    password);
}
```

12. Import the `NfcHelper.java` class into the project and enable the foreground dispatch system by overriding the `onResume` and `onPause` methods:

```java
@Override
protected void onResume() {
  super.onResume();

  if (nfcHelper.isNfcEnabledDevice()) {
  nfcHelper.enableForegroundDispatch();
  }
}

@Override
protected void onPause() {
  super.onPause();
```

```java
        if (nfcHelper.isNfcEnabledDevice()) {
          nfcHelper.disableForegroundDispatch();
        }
    }
}
```

13. Add the following class members to `MainActivity`:

```java
private NfcHelper nfcHelper;
private ProgressDialog waitingDialog;
private WifiNetwork wifiNetworkToWrite;
private boolean saveAsText;
private EditText txtSSID;
private EditText txtPassword;
private Spinner dropSecTypes;
```

14. Initialize `nfcHelper` and layout elements:

```java
@Override
protected void onCreate(Bundle savedInstanceState) {

    ...
nfcHelper = new NfcHelper(this);

txtSSID = (EditText) findViewById(R.id.txtSSID);
txtPassword = (EditText) findViewById(R.id.txtPassword);
dropSecTypes = (Spinner) findViewById(R.id.dropSecTypes);
}
```

15. Implement the `handleIntent` method:

```java
    private void handleIntent(Intent intent) {

      if (!nfcHelper.isNfcIntent(intent)) {
        return;
      }

    if (waitingDialog != null && wifiNetworkToWrite != null)
      {

        NdefMessage ndefMessage = null;

        if (!saveAsText) {

          ndefMessage = nfcHelper.
            createExternalTypeNdefMessage("ch9example2type",
              objectToBytes(wifiNetworkToWrite));

        } else {
```

```
        ndefMessage = nfcHelper.createTextNdefMessage
          (wifiNetworkToWrite.toString());

    }

    if (nfcHelper.writeNdefMessage(intent, ndefMessage))
      {
      Toast.makeText(this, R.string.toast_write_success,
        Toast.LENGTH_LONG).show();
    } else {
      Toast.makeText(this, R.string.toast_write_fail,
        Toast.LENGTH_LONG).show();
    }

    waitingDialog.dismiss();

  } else {

    NdefMessage ndefMessage =
      nfcHelper.getNdefMessageFromIntent(intent);
    NdefRecord ndefRecord =
      nfcHelper.getFirstNdefRecord(ndefMessage);

    WifiNetwork wifiNetwork = null;

    if (nfcHelper.isNdefRecordOfTnfAndRdt(ndefRecord,
      NdefRecord.TNF_WELL_KNOWN, NdefRecord.RTD_TEXT)) {

      wifiNetwork = new WifiNetwork
        (nfcHelper.getTextFromNdefRecord(ndefRecord));

    } else {

      wifiNetwork = (WifiNetwork) bytesToObject
        (ndefRecord.getPayload());

    }

    configureNetwork(wifiNetwork);

  }

}
```

16. Implement the `configureNetwork` method:

```
private void configureNetwork(WifiNetwork wifiNetwork) {

  WifiManager wifiManager = (WifiManager)
    this.getSystemService(Context.WIFI_SERVICE);
```

```java
    int networkId = wifiManager.
      addNetwork(wifiNetwork.getWifiConfiguration());

    wifiManager.enableNetwork(networkId, true);

    if (wifiManager.isWifiEnabled()) {
      wifiManager.reconnect();
    } else {
      wifiManager.setWifiEnabled(true);
    }

    Toast.makeText(this, wifiNetwork.getSsid() + "
      enabled!", Toast.LENGTH_LONG).show();

  }
```

17. Implement the `displayWaitingDialog` method:

```java
void displayWaitingDialog() {
  waitingDialog = new ProgressDialog(this);
  waitingDialog.setMessage(getString
    (R.string.dialog_waiting_tag));
  waitingDialog.setCancelable(true);
  waitingDialog.setOnDismissListener
    (new OnDismissListener() {

    @Override
    public void onDismiss(DialogInterface dialog) {

      waitingDialog = null;
      wifiNetworkToWrite = null;
      saveAsText = false;

    }
  });

  waitingDialog.show();
}
```

18. Implement the button click event listeners:

```java
public void onBtSaveClick(View view) {

  displayWaitingDialog();

  WifiNetwork wifiNetwork = new WifiNetwork();

  wifiNetwork.setSsid("" + txtSSID.getText());
  wifiNetwork.setPassword("" + txtPassword.getText());
  wifiNetwork.setSecurity("" +
    dropSecTypes.getSelectedItem());
```

```
      wifiNetworkToWrite = wifiNetwork;

  }

  public vcid onBtSaveAsTextClick(View view) {

    saveAsText = true;

    onBtSaveClick(view);
  }
```

19. Implement the `objectToBytes` and `bytesToObject` methods:

```
byte[] objectToBytes(Object obj) {
  ByteArrayOutputStream bos = new ByteArrayOutputStream();
  ObjectOutput out = null;

  try {
    out = new ObjectOutputStream(bos);
    out.writeObject(obj);

    out.close();
    bos.close();

  } catch (Exception e) {
    Log.e("objectToBytes", e.getMessage());
  }

  return bos.toByteArray();
}

Object bytesToObject(byte[] bytes) {
  Object o = null;
  ByteArrayInputStream bis = new
    ByteArrayInputStream(bytes);
  ObjectInput in = null;

  try {
    in = new ObjectInputStream(bis);

    o = in.readObject();

    bis.close();
  } catch (Exception e) {
    Log.e("bytesToObject", e.getMessage());
  }
  return o;
}
```

20. Call the `handleIntent` method to the `onResume` activity method:

```
@Override
protected void onResume() {

  ...

  handleIntent(getIntent());

}
```

21. Override the `onNewIntent` method:

```
@Override
  public void onNewIntent(Intent intent) {
    setIntent(intent);
}
```

22. Run the application, fill in the Wi-Fi network details, and choose **Write configs** or **Write configs (as plain text)**.

23. Tap the tag on your phone or simulate a tap in the NFC simulator to write the tag.

24. Tap again on the written tag. The network should be configured automatically and the Wi-Fi initiated.

How it works...

We encapsulate the Wi-Fi field values within the `WifiNetwork` class that contains all the logic related to the Wi-Fi network specs, and it is used to generate an instance of the `WifiConfiguration` class using the `getWifiConfiguration` method. This method is used when we add the network to our device using the `addNetwork` method from the `WifiManager` instance.

We store the Wi-Fi network in the tag in two different ways. In the first one, we convert `WifiNetwork` to a `byte[]` and store it. When we retrieve it, we simply convert it back to an instance of the `WifiNetwork` class. This approach is great because it eases our life as a developer, but besides the increased size of `NdefMessage`, it doesn't allow interoperability between applications. So, if we want several applications to recognize the data present in the tag, it would make perfect sense for multiple applications to recognize a Wi-Fi network setting. We need to adopt another strategy, so we save it as a concatenation of strings. It's not the perfect solution, but it will do the job.

Starting a Wi-Fi hotspot

The Android Wi-Fi hotspot feature is just incredible, and I can't help but love it! It allows me to have Internet access on my laptop everywhere. However, one thing that I don't like is the number of steps and the time needed to enable this feature. In this recipe, we will see how to reduce that time to just a few seconds and the steps to just one.

How to do it...

We will write a custom hotspot configuration and turn it on with one tap:

1. Open the project from the *Configuring a Wi-Fi network* recipe. Alternatively, create a new Android application project named `NfcBookCh9Example3` and package named `nfcbook.ch9.example3` and follow steps 2 through 20 from the previous recipe.

2. Replace the `network_sec_types` string array in the `res/values/strings.xml` file to allow only the creation of WPA networks:

```xml
<string-array name="network_sec_types">
    <item>WPA PSK</item>
</string-array>
```

3. Add the following `string` to the `res/values/strings.xml` file:

```xml
<string name="toast_wifi_ap_enabled">Wifi Ap
  enabled</string>
```

4. Implement the `getWifiApConfiguration` method in the `WifiNetwork` class:

```java
public WifiConfiguration getWifiApConfiguration() {

  WifiConfiguration wifiConfiguration = new
    WifiConfiguration();

  wifiConfiguration.SSID = ssid;

  wifiConfiguration.preSharedKey = password;
  wifiConfiguration.allowedKeyManagement.set
    (WifiConfiguration.KeyMgmt.WPA_PSK);
  wifiConfiguration.allowedProtocols.set
    (WifiConfiguration.Protocol.WPA);

  return wifiConfiguration;
}
```

5. Implement the `configureNetworkAp` method:

```java
private void configureNetworkAp(WifiNetwork wifiNetwork) {

  try {

    WifiManager wifiManager = (WifiManager) this.
      getSystemService(Context.WIFI_SERVICE);

    if (wifiManager.isWifiEnabled()) {
      wifiManager.setWifiEnabled(false);
    }
```

```java
        Method method = WifiManager.class.getMethod
          ("setWifiApEnabled", WifiConfiguration.class,
            boolean.class);

        method.invoke(wifiManager, wifiNetwork
          .getWifiApConfiguration(), true);

        Toast.makeText(this, R.string.toast_wifi_ap_enabled,
          Toast.LENGTH_LONG).show();

    } catch (Exception e) {

    }

  }
```

6. Call `configureNetworkAp` into the `handleIntent` method:

```java
    private void handleIntent(Intent intent) {

        if (!nfcHelper.isNfcIntent(intent)) {
          return;
        }

        if (waitingDialog != null && wifiNetworkToWrite !=
          null) {

          ...

        } else {

          NdefMessage ndefMessage = nfcHelper.
            getNdefMessageFromIntent(intent);
          NdefRecord ndefRecord =
            nfcHelper.getFirstNdefRecord(ndefMessage);

          WifiNetwork wifiNetwork = null;

          if (nfcHelper.isNdefRecordOfTnfAndRdt(ndefRecord,
            NdefRecord.TNF_WELL_KNOWN, NdefRecord.RTD_TEXT)) {

            wifiNetwork = new WifiNetwork
              (nfcHelper.getTextFromNdefRecord(ndefRecord));

          } else {

            wifiNetwork = (WifiNetwork)
              bytesToObject(ndefRecord.getPayload());

          }

          configureNetworkAp(wifiNetwork);

        }

    }
```

7. Run the application, fill in the Wi-Fi network details, and choose **Write configs** or **Write configs (as plain text)**.

8. Tap the tag on your phone or simulate a tap in the NFC simulator to write the tag.

9. Tap again on the written tag. The configured network app should start automatically.

How it works...

The Android SDK doesn't expose methods to configure and enable/disable the hotspot feature programmatically, but with a little magic from the `reflection` method, we can do it.

We need to get the private `setWifiApEnabled` method from the `WifiManager` class and invoke it using `reflection`. This method receives an instance of the `WifiConfiguration` class as shown in the previous recipe, but with subtle differences. In this case, we don't need to add the double quotes in the SSID or in the password. If we do this, the double quotes will be part of the SSID and password.

Inviting a friend to play a game – Part 2

In the *Inviting a friend to play a game – Part 1* recipe in *Chapter 7, Sharing Content across Devices*, we were able to share Bluetooth information between two devices. In Part 2, we will use that information to connect the devices and start a noughts and crosses game.

How to do it...

We will use the `BluetoothService` class to handle Bluetooth communication and send simple text messages between the devices:

1. Open Eclipse and create a new Android application project named `NfcBookCh9Example4` and package named `nfcbook.ch9.example4`.

2. Import the files from the *Inviting a friend to play a game – Part 1* recipe in *Chapter 7, Sharing Content across Devices*, or if preferred, continue following this recipe in the same project.

3. Make sure the `AndroidManifest.xml` file is correctly configured. Refer to the *Requesting NFC permissions* recipe in *Chapter 1, Getting Started with NFC*.

4. Import the `NfcHelper.java` class into the project.

5. Request for permission to administrate Bluetooth by adding the following lines of code to `AndroidManifest.xml`:

```xml
<uses-permission android:name="android.permission.
  BLUETOOTH_ADMIN" />
<uses-permission android:name=
  "android.permission.BLUETOOTH" />
```

6. Add the following `string` to the `res/values/strings.xml` file:

```xml
<string name="invite_friend_nfc">Invite friend over
  Nfc</string>
<string name="singleplayer">Singleplayer</string>
<string name="opponent">Opponent:</string>
<string name="button_reset">Reset</string>
<string name="dialog_waiting_opponent">Waiting for
  opponent</string>
<string name="toast_connection_lost">Connection was
  lost</string>
<string name="toast_unable_to_connect">Unable to
  connect</string>
```

7. Replace the content of the `activity_main.xml` file located at `/res/layout` with the following:

```xml
<RelativeLayout xmlns:android=
  "http://schemas.android.com/apk/res/android"
    xmlns:tools="http://schemas.android.com/tools"
    android:layout_width="match_parent"
    android:layout_height="match_parent"
    android:paddingBottom="@dimen/activity_vertical_margin"
    android:paddingLeft="@dimen/activity_horizontal_margin"
    android:paddingRight=
      "@dimen/activity_horizontal_margin"
    android:paddingTop="@dimen/activity_vertical_margin"
    tools:context=".MainActivity" >

    <Button
        android:id="@+id/btInviteNfc"
        android:layout_width="wrap_content"
        android:layout_height="wrap_content"
        android:layout_alignParentBottom="true"
        android:layout_alignParentLeft="true"
        android:layout_toLeftOf="@+id/btReset"
        android:onClick="onBtInviteNfcClick"
        android:text="@string/invite_friend_nfc" />

    <TextView
        android:id="@+id/textView1"
        android:layout_width="wrap_content"
        android:layout_height="wrap_content"
        android:layout_alignParentLeft="true"
```

```
            android:layout_alignParentTop="true"
            android:text="@string/opponent" />

    <TextView
        android:id="@+id/txtOpponentName"
        android:layout_width="wrap_content"
        android:layout_height="wrap_content"
        android:layout_alignBottom="@+id/textView1"
        android:layout_alignParentRight="true"
        android:layout_marginLeft="10dip"
        android:layout_toRightOf="@+id/textView1" />

    <TableLayout
        android:id="@+id/tableLayout1"
        android:layout_width="wrap_content"
        android:layout_height="wrap_content"
        android:layout_centerHorizontal="true"
        android:layout_centerVertical="true" >

        <TableRow
            android:layout_width="wrap_content"
            android:layout_height="wrap_content" >

            <Button
                android:layout_width="wrap_content"
                android:layout_height="wrap_content"
                android:visibility="invisible" />

            <View
                android:layout_width="1dp"
                android:layout_height="match_parent"
                android:background=
                  "@android:color/darker_gray" />

            <Button
                android:layout_width="wrap_content"
                android:layout_height="wrap_content"
                android:visibility="invisible" />

            <View
                android:layout_width="1dp"
                android:layout_height="match_parent"
                android:background=
                  "@android:color/darker_gray" />

            <Button
                android:layout_width="wrap_content"
```

```
            android:layout_height="wrap_content"
            android:visibility="invisible" />
    </TableRow>

    <TableRow
        android:id="@+id/tableRow1"
        android:layout_width="wrap_content"
        android:layout_height="wrap_content" >

        <Button
            android:id="@+id/bt0"
            android:layout_width="wrap_content"
            android:layout_height="wrap_content"
            android:enabled="false"
            android:onClick="onGameButtonClick"
            android:tag="0" />

        <View
            android:layout_width="1dp"
            android:layout_height="match_parent"
            android:background=
              "@android:color/darker_gray" />

        <Button
            android:id="@+id/bt1"
            android:layout_width="wrap_content"
            android:layout_height="wrap_content"
            android:enabled="false"
            android:onClick="onGameButtonClick"
            android:tag="1" />

        <View
            android:layout_width="1dp"
            android:layout_height="match_parent"
            android:background=
              "@android:color/darker_gray" />

        <Button
            android:id="@+id/bt2"
            android:layout_width="wrap_content"
            android:layout_height="wrap_content"
            android:enabled="false"
            android:onClick="onGameButtonClick"
            android:tag="2" />
    </TableRow>
```

```xml
<TableRow
    android:id="@+id/tableRow2"
    android:layout_width="wrap_content"
    android:layout_height="wrap_content" >

    <Button
        android:id="@+id/bt3"
        android:layout_width="wrap_content"
        android:layout_height="wrap_content"
        android:enabled="false"
        android:onClick="onGameButtonClick"
        android:tag="3" />

    <View
        android:layout_width="1dp"
        android:layout_height="match_parent"
        android:background=
            "@android:color/darker_gray" />

    <Button
        android:id="@+id/bt4"
        android:layout_width="wrap_content"
        android:layout_height="wrap_content"
        android:enabled="false"
        android:onClick="onGameButtonClick"
        android:tag="4" />

    <View
        android:layout_width="1dp"
        android:layout_height="match_parent"
        android:background=
            "@android:color/darker_gray" />

    <Button
        android:id="@+id/bt5"
        android:layout_width="wrap_content"
        android:layout_height="wrap_content"
        android:enabled="false"
        android:onClick="onGameButtonClick"
        android:tag="5" />
</TableRow>

<TableRow
    android:id="@+id/tableRow3"
    android:layout_width="wrap_content"
    android:layout_height="wrap_content" >
```

```xml
        <Button
            android:id="@+id/bt6"
            android:layout_width="wrap_content"
            android:layout_height="wrap_content"
            android:enabled="false"
            android:onClick="onGameButtonClick"
            android:tag="6" />

        <View
            android:layout_width="1dp"
            android:layout_height="match_parent"
            android:background=
              "@android:color/darker_gray" />

        <Button
            android:id="@+id/bt7"
            android:layout_width="wrap_content"
            android:layout_height="wrap_content"
            android:enabled="false"
            android:onClick="onGameButtonClick"
            android:tag="7" />

        <View
            android:layout_width="1dp"
            android:layout_height="match_parent"
            android:background=
              "@android:color/darker_gray" />

        <Button
            android:id="@+id/bt8"
            android:layout_width="wrap_content"
            android:layout_height="wrap_content"
            android:enabled="false"
            android:onClick="onGameButtonClick"
            android:tag="8" />
    </TableRow>

    <TableRow
        android:layout_width="wrap_content"
        android:layout_height="wrap_content" >

        <Button
            android:layout_width="wrap_content"
            android:layout_height="wrap_content"
            android:visibility="invisible" />
```

```xml
            <View
                android:layout_width="1dp"
                android:layout_height="match_parent"
                android:background=
                  "@android:color/darker_gray" />

            <Button
                android:layout_width="wrap_content"
                android:layout_height="wrap_content"
                android:visibility="invisible" />

            <View
                android:layout_width="1dp"
                android:layout_height="match_parent"
                android:background=
                  "@android:color/darker_gray" />

            <Button
                android:layout_width="wrap_content"
                android:layout_height="wrap_content"
                android:visibility="invisible" />
        </TableRow>
    </TableLayout>

    <View
        android:layout_width="match_parent"
        android:layout_height="1dp"
        android:layout_alignParentLeft="true"
        android:layout_alignTop="@+id/tableLayout1"
        android:layout_marginTop="96dp"
        android:background="@android:color/darker_gray" />

    <View
        android:id="@+id/view1"
        android:layout_width="match_parent"
        android:layout_height="1dp"
        android:layout_alignParentLeft="true"
        android:layout_alignTop="@+id/tableLayout1"
        android:layout_marginTop="144dp"
        android:background="@android:color/darker_gray" />

    <Button
        android:id="@+id/btReset"
        android:layout_width="wrap_content"
        android:layout_height="wrap_content"
        android:layout_alignParentBottom="true"
```

```
        android:layout_alignParentRight="true"
        android:enabled="false"
        android:onClick="onBtResetClick"
        android:text="@string/button_reset" />

</RelativeLayout>
```

8. This creates a layout identical to the following screenshot:

9. Create a new class file named `BluetoothService` and implement `ctor`:

```
public BluetoothService(Context context, Handler handler) {
mContext = context;
  mAdapter = BluetoothAdapter.getDefaultAdapter();
  mState = STATE_NONE;
  mHandler = handler;
}
```

10. Add the following class members to the `BluetoothService` class and the corresponding getters and setters:

```java
private static final String NAME_INSECURE =
  "BluetoothInsecure";
private static final UUID MY_UUID_INSECURE =
  UUID.fromString("bfd0c7d3-5dc2-48b5-a098-f341dc0f2372");

public static final int STATE_NONE = 0;
public static final int STATE_LISTEN = 1;
public static final int STATE_CONNECTING = 2;
public static final int STATE_CONNECTED = 3;

private final BluetoothAdapter mAdapter;
private final Handler mHandler;
private final Context mContext;
private AcceptThread mInsecureAcceptThread;
private ConnectThread mConnectThread;
private ConnectedThread mConnectedThread;
private int mState;


private synchronized void setState(int state) {
  mState = state;

  mHandler.obtainMessage(MainActivity.MESSAGE_STATE_CHANGE,
    state, -1).sendToTarget();
}

public synchronized int getState() {
  return mState;
}
```

11. Implement the `start` method:

```java
public synchronized void start() {

  cancelConnectThread();
  cancelConnectedThread();

  setState(STATE_LISTEN);

  if (mInsecureAcceptThread == null) {
    mInsecureAcceptThread = new AcceptThread(false);
    mInsecureAcceptThread.start();
  }
}
```

12. Implement the `connect` method:

```java
public synchronized void connect(BluetoothDevice device) {

    if (mState == STATE_CONNECTING) {
        cancelConnectThread();
    }

    cancelConnectedThread();

    mConnectThread = new ConnectThread(device);
    mConnectThread.start();
    setState(STATE_CONNECTING);
}
```

13. Implement the `connected` method:

```java
public synchronized void connected(BluetoothSocket socket,
BluetoothDevice device, final String socketType) {

    cancelConnectThread();
    cancelConnectedThread();
    cancelInsecureAcceptThread();

    mConnectedThread = new ConnectedThread(socket,
        socketType);
    mConnectedThread.start();

    Message msg = mHandler.obtainMessage
        (MainActivity.MESSAGE_DEVICE_NAME);
    Bundle bundle = new Bundle();
    bundle.putString(MainActivity.DEVICE_NAME,
        device.getName());
    msg.setData(bundle);
    mHandler.sendMessage(msg);

    setState(STATE_CONNECTED);
}
```

14. Implement the `stop` method:

```java
public synchronized void stop() {

    cancelConnectThread();
    cancelConnectedThread();
    cancelInsecureAcceptThread();

    setState(STATE_NONE);
}
```

15. Implement the `write` method:

```java
public void write(byte[] out) {

  ConnectedThread r;

  synchronized (this) {
    if (mState != STATE_CONNECTED)
      return;
    r = mConnectedThread;
  }

  r.write(out);
}
```

16. Implement the `sendMessage` method:

```java
private void sendMessage(int message) {
  Message msg = mHandler.obtainMessage
    (MainActivity.MESSAGE_TOAST);
  Bundle bundle = new Bundle();
  bundle.putString(MainActivity.TOAST,
    mContext.getString(message));
  msg.setData(bundle);
  mHandler.sendMessage(msg);

  BluetoothService.this.start();
}
```

17. Override the `cancelConnectThread`, `cancelConnectedThread`, and `cancelInsecureAcceptThread` methods:

```java
private void cancelConnectThread() {
  if (mConnectThread != null) {
    mConnectThread.cancel();
    mConnectThread = null;
  }
}

private void cancelConnectedThread() {

  if (mConnectedThread != null) {
    mConnectedThread.cancel();
    mConnectedThread = null;
  }
}

private void cancelInsecureAcceptThread() {
  if (mInsecureAcceptThread != null) {
```

```
      mInsecureAcceptThread.cancel();
      mInsecureAcceptThread = null;
    }
  }
```

18. Implement the `AcceptThread` class thread in the `BluetoothService` class:

```
private class AcceptThread extends Thread {
  private final BluetoothServerSocket mmServerSocket;
  private String mSocketType;

  public AcceptThread(boolean secure) {
    BluetoothServerSocket tmp = null;
    mSocketType = "Insecure";

    try {
      tmp = mAdapter.
        listenUsingInsecureRfcommWithServiceRecord
          (NAME_INSECURE, MY_UUID_INSECURE);

    } catch (IOException e) {

    }
    mmServerSocket = tmp;
  }

  public void run() {
    setName("AcceptThread" + mSocketType);

    BluetoothSocket socket = null;

    while (mState != STATE_CONNECTED) {
      try {
        socket = mmServerSocket.accept();
      } catch (IOException e) {

        break;
      }

      if (socket != null) {
        synchronized (BluetoothService.this) {
          switch (mState) {
          case STATE_LISTEN:
          case STATE_CONNECTING:
            connected(socket, socket.getRemoteDevice(),
              mSocketType);
            break;
```

```
            case STATE_NONE:
            case STATE_CONNECTED:
              try {
                socket.close();
                } catch (IOException e) {

              }
              break;
              }
            ;

          }
        }

      }

    public void cancel() {
      try {
        mmServerSocket.close();
      } catch (IOException e) {

      }
    }
  }
```

19. Implement the `ConnectThread` thread in the `BluetoothService` class:

```
private class ConnectThread extends Thread {
  private final BluetoothSocket mmSocket;
  private final BluetoothDevice mmDevice;
  private String mSocketType;

  public ConnectThread(BluetoothDevice device) {
    mmDevice = device;
    BluetoothSocket tmp = null;
    mSocketType = "Insecure";

    try {
      tmp = device.
        createInsecureRfcommSocketToServiceRecord
          (MY_UUID_INSECURE);

    } catch (IOException e) {

    }
    mmSocket = tmp;
  }

  public void run() {
    setName("ConnectThread" + mSocketType);
```

```
    mAdapter.cancelDiscovery();

    try {
      mmSocket.connect();
    } catch (IOException e) {

      try {
        mmSocket.close();
      } catch (IOException e2) {

      }

      sendMessage(R.string.toast_unable_to_connect);

      return;
    }

    synchronized (BluetoothService.this) {
      mConnectThread = null;
    }

    connected(mmSocket, mmDevice, mSocketType);
  }

  public void cancel() {
    try {
      mmSocket.close();
    } catch (IOException e) {

    }
  }
}
```

20. Implement the `ConnectedThread` thread in the `BluetoothService` class:

```
private class ConnectedThread extends Thread {
  private final BluetoothSocket mmSocket;
  private final InputStream mmInStream;
  private final OutputStream mmOutStream;

  public ConnectedThread(BluetoothSocket socket,
    String socketType) {

    mmSocket = socket;
    InputStream tmpIn = null;
    OutputStream tmpOut = null;

    try {
      tmpIn = socket.getInputStream();
      tmpOut = socket.getOutputStream();
```

```java
        } catch (IOException e) {

        }

      mmInStream = tmpIn;
      mmOutStream = tmpOut;
    }

    public void run() {

      byte[] buffer = new byte[1024];
      int bytes;

      while (true) {
        try {

          bytes = mmInStream.read(buffer);

        mHandler.obtainMessage(MainActivity.MESSAGE_READ,
          bytes, -1, buffer).sendToTarget();
        } catch (IOException e) {

          sendMessage(R.string.toast_connection_lost);

          BluetoothService.this.start();
          break;
        }
      }
    }

    public void write(byte[] buffer) {
      try {
        mmOutStream.write(buffer);

        mHandler.obtainMessage(MainActivity.MESSAGE_WRITE,
          -1, -1, buffer).sendToTarget();
      } catch (IOException e) {

      }
    }

    public void cancel() {
      try {
        mmSocket.close();
      } catch (IOException e) {

      }
    }
  }
```

21. Add the following class members to `MainActivity`:

```java
public static final int MESSAGE_STATE_CHANGE = 1;
public static final int MESSAGE_READ = 2;
public static final int MESSAGE_WRITE = 3;
public static final int MESSAGE_DEVICE_NAME = 4;
public static final int MESSAGE_TOAST = 5;
public static final String TOAST = "toast";
public static final String DEVICE_NAME = "device_name";

private BluetoothAdapter btAdapter;
private NfcHelper nfcHelper;
private Handler handler;
private Handler bluetoothHandler;
private ProgressDialog waitingDialog;
private BluetoothService bluetoothService;

private String myGameIdentifier = "O";
private String friendGameIdentifier = "X";
private Button btInviteNfc;
private Button btReset;
private Player player;
private TextView txtOpponentName;
```

22. Override the `onCreate` method:

```java
@Override
protected void onCreate(Bundle savedInstanceState) {
    super.onCreate(savedInstanceState);
    setContentView(R.layout.activity_main);

    btAdapter = BluetoothAdapter.getDefaultAdapter();
    nfcHelper = new NfcHelper(this);

    btInviteNfc = (Button) findViewById(R.id.btInviteNfc);
    btReset = (Button) findViewById(R.id.btReset);
    txtOpponentName = ((TextView) findViewById
        (R.id.txtOpponentName));

    initHandlers();

    bluetoothService = new BluetoothService
        (this, bluetoothHandler);

    if (btAdapter == null || !btAdapter.isEnabled()) {
        Toast.makeText(this, "Bluetooth not available or
            disabled", Toast.LENGTH_SHORT).show();
```

```
        finish();
        return;
      }
    }
```

23. Implement the `initHandlers` method:

```java
private void initHandlers() {
  handler = new Handler() {
    @Override
    public void handleMessage(Message msg) {

      Toast.makeText(getApplicationContext(), "Beam sent!",
        Toast.LENGTH_LONG).show();

    }
  };

  bluetoothHandler = new Handler() {
    @Override
    public void handleMessage(Message msg) {

      switch (msg.what) {
      case MESSAGE_STATE_CHANGE:
        switch (msg.arg1) {
        case BluetoothService.STATE_CONNECTED:
          initGame();
          break;
        case BluetoothService.STATE_CONNECTING:
          break;
        case BluetoothService.STATE_LISTEN:
        case BluetoothService.STATE_NONE:

          btInviteNfc.setEnabled(true);
          btReset.setEnabled(false);
          txtOpponentName.setText("");

          break;
        }
        break;

      case MESSAGE_DEVICE_NAME:
        String connectedDeviceName =
          msg.getData().getString(DEVICE_NAME);

        if (player == null) {
          player = new Player();
          player.setName(connectedDeviceName);
        }
```

```java
      break;

case MESSAGE_TOAST:
  Toast.makeText(getApplicationContext(),
    msg.getData().getString(TOAST),
      Toast.LENGTH_SHORT).show();
  break;

case MESSAGE_WRITE:

  byte[] writeBuf = (byte[]) msg.obj;
  String writeMessage = new String(writeBuf);

  if (writeMessage.equals("reset")) {

    initGame();

  } else {

    int playedButtonId = getResources().
      getIdentifier("bt" + writeMessage, "id",
        getPackageName());
    Button playedButton = ((Button)
      findViewById(playedButtonId));

    playedButton.setText(myGameIdentifier);
    playedButton.setEnabled(false);
  }
  break;

case MESSAGE_READ:
  byte[] readBuf = (byte[]) msg.obj;
  String readMessage = new String(readBuf, 0,
    msg.arg1);

  if (readMessage.equals("reset")) {
    initGame();
  } else {

    int friendPlayedAtButtonId =
      getResources().getIdentifier("bt" +
        readMessage, "id", getPackageName());
    Button friendPlayedAtButton = ((Button)
      findViewById(friendPlayedAtButtonId));
    friendPlayedAtButton.setText
      (friendGameIdentifier);
    friendPlayedAtButton.setEnabled(false);

  }
```

```java
            break;
        }
    }
};

}
```

24. Implement the `initGame` method:

```java
private void initGame() {

    for (int i = 0; i < 9; i++) {

        int id = getResources().getIdentifier("bt" + i, "id",
getPackageName());
        Button button = (Button) findViewById(id);

        button.setEnabled(true);
        button.setText("");

    }

    btInviteNfc.setEnabled(false);
    btReset.setEnabled(true);

    txtOpponentName.setText(player.getName());

}
```

25. Implement the button click event listeners:

```java
public void onGameButtonClick(View v) {
    bluetoothService.write(v.getTag().toString().getBytes());
}

public void onBtResetClick(View v) {
    bluetoothService.write("reset".getBytes());
}
```

26. Run the application and click on **Invite friend over NFC**.

27. A connected toast and the name of your opponent should appear.

Have fun!

How it works...

The key piece of the puzzle in this recipe is the `BluetoothService` class. It is responsible for starting the threads that enable listening for connections using `AcceptThread`, establishing the connections using `ConnectThread`, and exchanging messages using `ConnectedThread`. When the application starts, we call the `start` method, which allows our device to start listening for the connection requests. We only try to establish a connection when we receive the incoming NFC beam that contains the other device's Bluetooth address by calling the `connect` method. This method tries to create a **radio frequency communication** (**RFCOMM**) socket between the devices.

When the connection is established, we call the `write` method to send text content between the devices. When the user taps the button at position 1 x 1, the message sent is `0`; for the position 1 x 2, the message is `1`; for the position 2 x 2, it is `4`; and so on. Additionally, we send a `reset` command to reinitialize the game.

Controlling hotel room access with Arduino and NFC – Part 1

Imagine you are at a hotel where each lock to the rooms is controlled by Arduino with an NFC shield. When you arrive at your room and place the NFC card against the reader, Arduino will validate if it is indeed the correct card before releasing the lock.

In this recipe, we will create an Android application to write the room number on an NFC card encrypted with an AES algorithm.

How to do it...

We will encrypt the room door (padded left with `0` to have `16` as the length) with a 32-bit key and save the result to the tag:

1. Open Eclipse and create a new Android application project named `NfcBookCh9Example5` and package named `nfcbook.ch9.example5`.

2. Make sure the `AndroidManifest.xml` file is correctly configured. Refer to the *Requesting NFC permissions* recipe in *Chapter 1, Getting Started with NFC*.

3. Add the following `string` to the `res/values/strings.xml` file:

```
<string name="dialog_waiting_tag">Waiting tag...</string>
<string name="label_aes_key">AES key</string>
<string name="label_room_number">Room number</string>
<string name="label_output">Ouput</string>
<string name="button_write">Write</string>
<string name="button_new_key">new key</string>
```

```
<string name="toast_write_success">Tag written</string>
<string name="toast_write_fail">Failed to write tag</string>
<string name="text_aes_key">
    1wQ8rcCtkjpHALVphJJxMHS4a3/ZOuuJg8V7i/ucaqk=</string>
```

4. Replace the content of the `activity_main.xml` file located at `/res/layout` with the following:

```xml
<RelativeLayout xmlns:android=
  "http://schemas.android.com/apk/res/android"
    xmlns:tools="http://schemas.android.com/tools"
    android:layout_width="match_parent"
    android:layout_height="match_parent"
    android:orientation="vertical"
    android:paddingBottom="@dimen/activity_vertical_margin"
    android:paddingLeft="@dimen/activity_horizontal_margin"
    android:paddingRight=
      "@dimen/activity_horizontal_margin"
    android:paddingTop="@dimen/activity_vertical_margin"
    tools:context=".MainActivity" >

    <TextView
        android:id="@+id/textView1"
        android:layout_width="wrap_content"
        android:layout_height="wrap_content"
        android:layout_alignParentLeft="true"
        android:text="@string/label_aes_key" />

    <Button
        android:id="@+id/btWriteTag"
        android:layout_width="wrap_content"
        android:layout_height="wrap_content"
        android:layout_alignParentBottom="true"
        android:layout_alignParentLeft="true"
        android:layout_alignParentRight="true"
        android:text="@string/button_write"
        android:onClick="onBtWriteTagClick"/>

    <EditText
        android:id="@+id/txtAesKey"
        android:layout_width="match_parent"
        android:layout_height="wrap_content"
        android:layout_alignParentLeft="true"
        android:layout_alignParentRight="true"
        android:layout_below="@+id/textView1"
        android:ems="10"
        android:text="@string/text_aes_key" >
```

```xml
        <requestFocus />
    </EditText>

    <Button
        android:id="@+id/btNewKey"
        android:layout_width="wrap_content"
        android:layout_height="wrap_content"
        android:layout_alignParentLeft="true"
        android:layout_alignRight="@+id/txtAesKey"
        android:layout_below="@+id/txtAesKey"
        android:text="@string/button_new_key"
        android:onClick="onBtNewKeyClick"/>

    <TextView
        android:id="@+id/textView2"
        android:layout_width="wrap_content"
        android:layout_height="wrap_content"
        android:layout_alignLeft="@+id/btNewKey"
        android:layout_below="@+id/btNewKey"
        android:layout_marginTop="20dip"
        android:text="@string/label_room_number" />

    <EditText
        android:id="@+id/txtRoomNumber"
        android:layout_width="match_parent"
        android:layout_height="wrap_content"
        android:layout_alignParentLeft="true"
        android:layout_below="@+id/textView2"
        android:ems="10"
        android:inputType="number" />

    <TextView
        android:id="@+id/textView3"
        android:layout_width="wrap_content"
        android:layout_height="wrap_content"
        android:layout_alignLeft="@+id/txtRoomNumber"
        android:layout_below="@+id/txtRoomNumber"
        android:layout_marginTop="20dip"
        android:text="@string/label_output" />

    <EditText
        android:id="@+id/txtOutput"
        android:layout_width="match_parent"
        android:layout_height="wrap_content"
        android:layout_alignParentLeft="true"
        android:layout_below="@+id/textView3"
```

```
            android:editable="false"
            android:ems="10" />

    </RelativeLayout>
```

5. This creates a layout identical to that in the following screenshot:

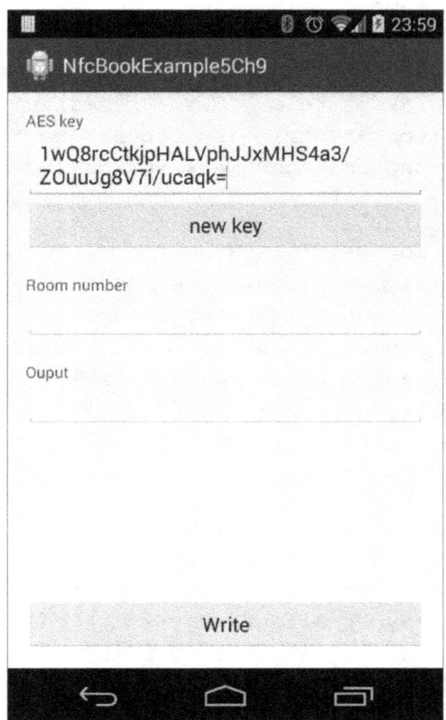

6. Import the `NfcHelper.java` class into the project and enable the foreground dispatch system by overriding the `onResume` and `onPause` methods:

```
@Override
protected void onResume() {
  super.onResume();

  if (nfcHelper.isNfcEnabledDevice()) {
    nfcHelper.enableForegroundDispatch();
  }
}

@Override
protected void onPause() {
  super.onPause();
```

```java
    if (nfcHelper.isNfcEnabledDevice()) {
      nfcHelper.disableForegroundDispatch();
    }
  }
}
```

7. Implement the `TextWatcher` interface in the `MainActivity` file:

```java
public class MainActivity extends Activity implements
  TextWatcher {
  ...
  @Override
  public void onTextChanged(CharSequence s, int start, int
    before, int count) {

  try {

      if (txtRoomNumber.getText().toString().isEmpty()) {
        txtOutput.setText("");
      } else {

      String roomNumber = String.format("%016d",
        Integer.parseInt("" + txtRoomNumber.getText()));

        txtOutput.setText("" + encrypt("" + txtAesKey.getText(),
          "" + roomNumber));
      }
    } catch (Exception e) {

    }
  }
}
```

8. Add the following class members to `MainActivity`:

```java
private static final String algorithm = "AES/ECB/NoPadding";
private NfcHelper nfcHelper;
private ProgressDialog waitingDialog;
private TextView txtAesKey;
private TextView txtRoomNumber;
private TextView txtOutput;
```

9. Initialize the class members:

```java
@Override
protected void onCreate(Bundle savedInstanceState) {

  ...
  txtAesKey = (TextView) findViewById(R.id.txtAesKey);
  txtRoomNumber = (TextView)
    findViewById(R.id.txtRoomNumber);
```

```java
        txtOutput = (TextView) findViewById(R.id.txtOutput);

        txtRoomNumber.addTextChangedListener(this);

        nfcHelper = new NfcHelper(this);

    }
```

10. Implement the `handleIntent` method:

```java
    private void handleIntent(Intent intent) {

      if (!nfcHelper.isNfcIntent(intent)) {
        return;
      }

      try {

        if (waitingDialog != null) {

          NdefMessage ndefMessage =
            nfcHelper.createTextNdefMessage("" +
              txtOutput.getText());

          if (nfcHelper.writeNdefMessage(intent,
            ndefMessage)) {
            Toast.makeText(this, R.string.
              toast_write_success, Toast.LENGTH_LONG).show();
          } else {
            Toast.makeText(this, R.string.toast_write_fail,
              Toast.LENGTH_LONG).show();
          }

          waitingDialog.dismiss();
          waitingDialog = null;

        } else {

          NdefMessage ndefMessage =
            nfcHelper.getNdefMessageFromIntent(intent);
          NdefRecord ndefRecord =
            nfcHelper.getFirstNdefRecord(ndefMessage);

          String encryptedRoom =
            nfcHelper.getTextFromNdefRecord(ndefRecord);

          Toast.makeText(this, decrypt("" +
            txtAesKey.getText(), encryptedRoom),
              Toast.LENGTH_LONG).show();

        }

      } catch (Exception e) {
```

```
Log.e("handleIntent", e.toString());
    }
  }
```

11. Implement the `generateKey` method:

```
private String generateKey() throws
  NoSuchAlgorithmException {
  KeyGenerator generator;
  generator = KeyGenerator.getInstance("AES");
  generator.init(256);

  SecretKey key = generator.generateKey();

  return Base64.encodeToString(key.getEncoded(),
    Base64.DEFAULT);
}
```

12. Implement the `encrypt` method:

```
private String encrypt(String key, String message) throws
  Exception {
  byte[] encodedKey = Base64.decode(key, Base64.DEFAULT);

  SecretKeySpec skeySpec = new SecretKeySpec(encodedKey,
    algorithm);
  Cipher cipher = Cipher.getInstance(algorithm);

  cipher.init(Cipher.ENCRYPT_MODE, skeySpec);

  byte[] messageBytes = message.getBytes("UTF8");
  byte[] encrypted = cipher.doFinal(messageBytes);

  return Base64.encodeToString(encrypted, Base64.DEFAULT);
}
```

13. Implement the `decrypt` method:

```
private String decrypt(String key, String encryptedMessage)
  throws Exception {
  byte[] encodedKey = Base64.decode(key, Base64.DEFAULT);
  SecretKeySpec skeySpec = new SecretKeySpec(encodedKey,
    algorithm);
  Cipher cipher = Cipher.getInstance(algorithm);
  cipher.init(Cipher.DECRYPT_MODE, skeySpec);

  byte[] encryptedMessageBytes =
    Base64.decode(encryptedMessage, Base64.DEFAULT);
  byte[] decrypted = cipher.doFinal(encryptedMessageBytes);

  return new String(decrypted, "UTF8");
}
```

14. Implement the button click event listeners:

```java
public void onBtWriteTagClick(View view) {

    waitingDialog = new ProgressDialog(this);
    waitingDialog.setMessage(getString
        (R.string.dialog_waiting_tag));
    waitingDialog.setCancelable(true);

    waitingDialog.show();

}

public void onBtNewKeyClick(View view) {
    try {

        txtAesKey.setText(generateKey());

    } catch (Exception e) {

    }
}
```

15. Call the `handleIntent` method in the `onResume` activity method:

```java
@Override
protected void onResume() {
    ...

    handleIntent(getIntent());

}
```

16. Override the `onNewIntent` method:

```java
@Override
public void onNewIntent(Intent intent) {
    setIntent(intent);
}
```

17. Run the application and type in the room number to be encrypted and written on the NFC card.

18. Tap the card on your phone or simulate a tap in the NFC simulator to write on the card.

How it works...

We use the AES algorithm with no padding, which means we can only encrypt a fixed length of data, that is, 16 bits. We add zeroes to the left of the input room number (I can't imagine a hotel with more than 9999999999999999 rooms!) to make it always 16 bits in length. Now that we have the complete room number, we encrypt it using a generated AES-32 bit key and the output is written into the tag after being base64 encoded for a more friendly representation. The key used to write the cards needs to be the same in Arduino or the output will be different, and therefore the door won't open.

Controlling hotel room access with Arduino and NFC – Part 2

In this recipe, we create an Arduino application that will read the encrypted data from the NFC card and compare it with the room number it has been configured to.

Getting ready

We assume that an Arduino ship has been connected properly with an Adafruit NFC shield and that the Arduino software and drivers are correctly installed and working.

How to do it...

We will retrieve the data from the tag and compare it with the encrypted room number:

1. Download the `arduino_NFC` library from `https://github.com/odopod/arduino_NFC`.

2. Download `AESLib` from `https://github.com/DavyLandman/AESLib`.

3. Download the `arduino-base64` library from `https://github.com/adamvr/arduino-base64`.

4. Navigate to the Arduino software installation directory and extract both downloaded libraries to the folder libraries.

5. Open the Arduino software and create a new script. Navigate to **Sketch | Import Library...**, where both libraries should be present as shown in the following screenshot:

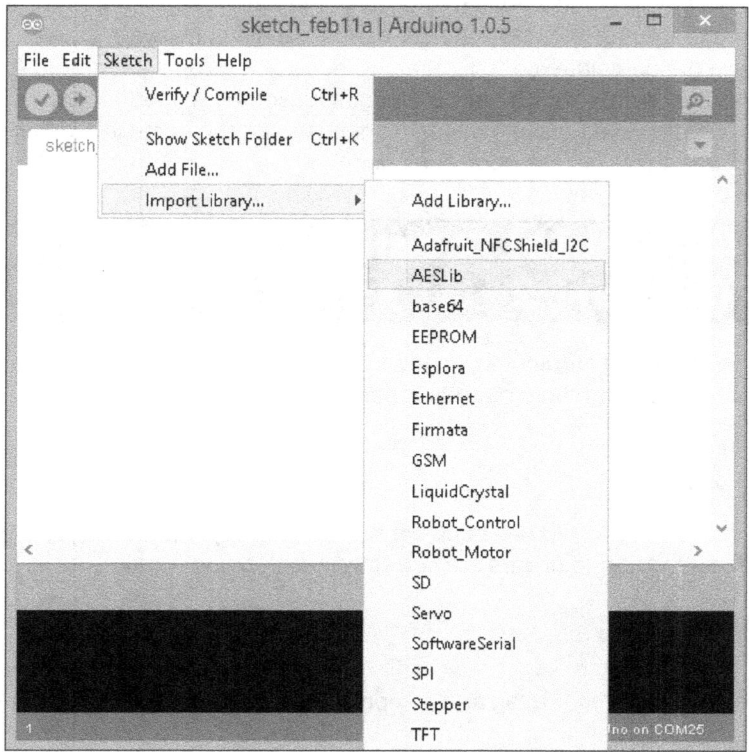

6. Paste the following code:

```
#include <Base64.h>
#include <AESLib.h>
#include <Wire.h>

#include <PN532_I2C.h>

#define IRQ   2
#define RESET 3

PN532 * board = new PN532_I2C(IRQ, RESET);

#include <Mifare.h>
Mifare mifare;
//init keys for reading classic
uint8_t Mifare::useKey = KEY_A;
```

```cpp
uint8_t Mifare::keyA[6] = {0xD3, 0xF7, 0xD3, 0xF7, 0xD3,
  0xF7 };
uint8_t Mifare::keyB[6] = {0xFF, 0xFF, 0xFF, 0xFF, 0xFF,
  0xFF };
uint32_t Mifare::cardType = 0; //will get overwritten if it
  finds a different card

#include <NDEF.h>

#define PAYLOAD_SIZE 224
uint8_t payload[PAYLOAD_SIZE] = {};

void setup(void) {
  Serial.begin(115200);

  board->begin();

  uint32_t versiondata = board->getFirmwareVersion();
  if (! versiondata) {
      Serial.print("Didn't find PN53x board");
      while (1);
  }

  Serial.print("Found chip PN5");
  Serial.println((versiondata >> 24) & 0xFF, HEX);
  Serial.print("Firmware ver. ");
  Serial.print((versiondata >> 16) & 0xFF, DEC);
  Serial.print('.');
  Serial.println((versiondata >> 8) & 0xFF, DEC);

  mifare.SAMConfig();

}

void loop(void) {
 uint8_t * uid;

  Serial.println("Waiting for tag...");
  do {
    uid = mifare.readTarget();
  }
  while (!uid);
  Serial.println("Tag found!");

  Serial.println(Mifare::cardType == MIFARE_CLASSIC ?
    "Classic" : "Ultralight");
```

```cpp
  memset(payload, 0, PAYLOAD_SIZE);

  //read
  mifare.readPayload(payload, PAYLOAD_SIZE);

  FOUND_MESSAGE m = NDEF().decode_message(payload);

  if(m.type == NDEF_TYPE_TEXT){

    validateRoomNumberAndOpenDoor((char*)m.payload);

  }else{
    Serial.println("Unrecognized content.");
  }

  delay(5000);
}

void validateRoomNumberAndOpenDoor(char* data) {
  //byte[] representation of our AES key generated in the
    Android app
  uint8_t key[] = {
      -41,4,60,-83,-64,-83,-110,58,71,0,-75,105,-124,-
    110,113,48,116,-72,107,127,-39,58,-21,-119,-125,-
      59,123,-117,-5,-100,106,-87
  };
  char roomNumber[] = "0000000000000101";
  char roomEncoded[24];
  aes256_enc_single(key, roomNumber);

  base64_encode(roomEncoded, roomNumber, 16);

  int result = 1;
  int dataLen = strlen(data);

  if( dataLen - 1 != 24 ){
    result = 0;
  }else{

    int i;
    for(i = 0; i<24; i++){
      if(data[i] != roomEncoded[i]){
       result = 0;
       i=24;
      }
    }
  }

}
```

```
if(  result == 1 ) {
  Serial.println("Room number matched card value! Opening
    door.");
} else {
  Serial.println("Wrong room!");
}


}
```

7. Connect Arduino, upload the script, and open the serial monitor.

8. Tap the previously written tag that contains the encrypted room number.

9. If the room number matches `101`, the **Room number matched card value! Opening door** message should appear.

How it works...

To read the tag content, we used the same code from the previous recipes. Here, the difference is in the `validateRoomNumberAndOpenDoor` method. In this method, we have `roomNumber` and `key`. The `roomNumber` command will be different for each room and the `key` command needs to be the same as that used in the write operation for the NFC card.

The `validateRoomNumberAndOpenDoor` method receives a `data` parameter, which is the encrypted room number present on the card. To check if this card is for this room, we encrypt the value present in the `roomNumber` variable by calling the `aes256_enc_single` method. Since the tag content is base64 encoded, we also need to encode the result of the encryption method by calling `base64_encode`. After that, we just need to compare both encrypted and encoded strings, and if they match, we release the door lock.

Don't forget to import the `AESLib` and `Arduino-base64` libraries or we can't use the `aes256_enc_single` and `base64_encode` methods.

10
Real-life Examples – NFC Utilities

In this chapter, we will cover the following topics:

- Creating multi-action tags
- Choosing the best format for our data
- Locking tags
- Joking with a friend

Introduction

In this final chapter, we will use the knowledge we gathered on reading and writing tags to create more complete applications and cover some suggestions on how to store our data, how to lock tags, and have some fun with NFC.

Creating multi-action tags

In this recipe, we will create a basic application that allows us to take advantage of the `NdefMessage` structure to write multiple actions to a tag.

Getting ready

You will need the following prerequisites while creating multi-action tags:

- Make sure you have a working Android development environment. If you don't, ADT Bundle is a good kit to start with (`http://developer.android.com/sdk/index.html`).

- Make sure you have an NFC-enabled Android device or a virtual test environment. Refer to the *Testing your app all together* recipe in *Chapter 1, Getting Started with NFC*.

- It will be assumed that Eclipse is the development IDE and that you are familiar with writing external type `NdefRecord`. Refer to the *Working with external types* recipe in *Chapter 3, Writing Tag Content*.

How to do it...

We will write a `byte` value that represents an `enum` item. This `enum` item contains several pre-programmed actions. Switch Wi-Fi and Bluetooth on and off, navigate to `www.packtpub.com`, and open the PacktPub Reader app. When the tag is read, the application will perform the saved actions in the order they were written. Perform the following steps:

1. Open Eclipse and create a new Android application project named `NfcBookCh10Example1` and a package named `com.nfcbook.ch10.example1`.

2. Make sure the `AndroidManifest.xml` file is configured correctly. Refer to the *Requesting NFC permissions* recipe in *Chapter 1, Getting Started with NFC*.

3. Request permissions to change the Wi-Fi and Bluetooth adapter's state by adding the following lines of code to `AndroidManifest.xml`:

```xml
<uses-permission
    android:name="android.permission.BLUETOOTH" />
<uses-permission
    android:name="android.permission.ACCESS_WIFI_STATE" />
<uses-permission
    android:name="android.permission.CHANGE_WIFI_STATE" />
<uses-permission
    android:name="android.permission.BLUETOOTH_ADMIN" />
```

4. Set the minimum SDK version to `16` using the following code:

```xml
<uses-sdk android:minSdkVersion="16" />
```

5. Add the following `intent-filter` tag to `MainActivity` in the `AndroidManifest` file using the following code:

```xml
<intent-filter>
    <action android:name="android.nfc.action.NDEF_DISCOVERED"
      />
```

```xml
<category android:name="android.intent.category.DEFAULT"
  />

<data
  android:host="ext"
  android:pathPrefix="/com.packtpub:ch10example1type"
  android:scheme="vnd.android.nfc" />
</intent-filter>
```

6. Add the following strings to the `strings.xml` file located at `res/values/`:

```xml
<string name="selected_actions">Selected actions:</string>
<string name="actions">Actions</string>
<string name="write_tag">Write tag</string>
<string name="dialog_waiting_tag">Waiting tag...</string>
<string name="toast_write_success">Tag written</string>
<string name="toast_write_fail">Failed to write
  tag</string>
  <string-array name="actions">
    <item>None</item>
    <item>Enable wifi</item>
    <item>Disable wifi</item>
    <item>Enable bluetooth</item>
    <item>Disable bluetooth</item>
    <item>Navigate to packtpub.com</item>
    <item>Open Packt Reader Application</item>
  </string-array>
```

7. Replace the content of the `activity_main.xml` file located at `/res/layout` with the following code:

```xml
<LinearLayout xmlns:android=
  "http://schemas.android.com/apk/res/android"
    xmlns:tools="http://schemas.android.com/tools"
    xmlns:app="http://schemas.android.com/apk/res-auto"
    android:layout_width="match_parent"
    android:layout_height="match_parent"
    android:orientation="vertical"
    android:paddingBottom="@dimen/activity_vertical_margin"
    android:paddingLeft="@dimen/activity_horizontal_margin"
    android:paddingRight=
      "@dimen/activity_horizontal_margin"
    android:paddingTop="@dimen/activity_vertical_margin"
    tools:context=".MainActivity">
```

```xml
<TextView
  android:id="@+id/textView1"
  android:layout_width="wrap_content"
  android:layout_height="wrap_content"
  android:text="@string/actions" />

<Spinner
  android:id="@+id/spinnerAction"
  android:layout_width="fill_parent"
  android:layout_height="wrap_content"
  android:prompt="@string/actions"
  android:entries="@array/actions"/>

<TextView
  android:id="@+id/textView2"
  android:layout_width="wrap_content"
  android:layout_height="wrap_content"
  android:layout_marginTop="20dip"
  android:text="@string/selected_actions" />

<ListView
  android:id="@+id/lstSelectedActions"
  android:layout_width="match_parent"
  android:layout_height="0dip"
  android:layout_weight="1" >
</ListView>

<Button
  android:id="@+id/btnWriteTag"
  android:layout_width="match_parent"
  android:layout_height="wrap_content"
  android:text="@string/write_tag"
  android:onClick="onBtnWriteTagClick" />

</LinearLayout>
```

The preceding code creates a layout that is identical to that in the following screenshot:

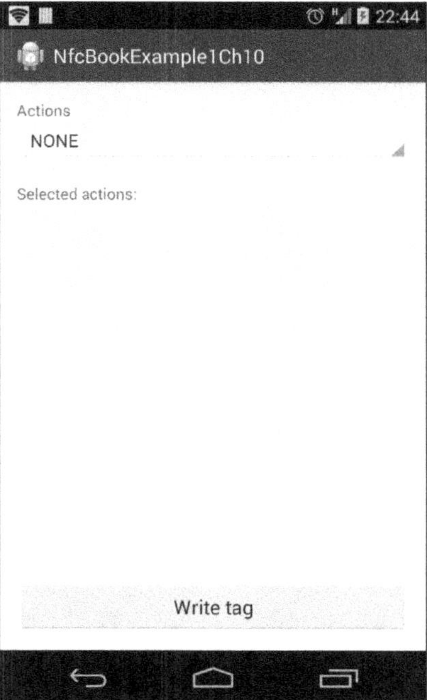

8. Create a new class file named `ActionHelper` and implement the following constructor:

```java
public ActionHelper(Context context) {

    this.context = context;

    this.wifiManager = (WifiManager)
        context.getSystemService(Context.WIFI_SERVICE);
    this.bluetoothAdapter =
        BluetoothAdapter.getDefaultAdapter();

}
```

9. Add the following class fields to the `AdapterHelper` class:

```java
private Context context;
private WifiManager wifiManager;
private BluetoothAdapter bluetoothAdapter;
```

10. Add the following `enum` item to the `ActionHelper` class:

```java
public enum Actions {
  NONE,
  WIFI_ON,
  WIFI_OFF,
  BLUETOOTH_ON,
  BLUETOOTH_OFF,
  NAVIGATE_TO_PACKT_PUB,
  OPEN_PACKT_READER_APP
}
```

11. Implement the methods to change the Wi-Fi states as follows:

```java
public void enableWifi() {

  if (!wifiManager.isWifiEnabled()) {
    wifiManager.setWifiEnabled(true);
  }

}


public void disableWifi() {

  if (!wifiManager.isWifiEnabled()) {
    wifiManager.setWifiEnabled(false);
  }

}
```

12. Implement the methods to change the Bluetooth states as follows:

```java
public void enableBluetooth() {
  if (bluetoothAdapter != null &&
    !bluetoothAdapter.isEnabled()) {
    bluetoothAdapter.enable();
  }
}


public void disableBluetooth() {
  if (bluetoothAdapter != null &&
    bluetoothAdapter.isEnabled()) {
    bluetoothAdapter.disable();
  }
}
```

13. Implement the methods to navigate to a URL as follows:

```java
public void navigateToUrl(String url) {
  Intent browserIntent = new Intent(Intent.ACTION_VIEW,
    Uri.parse(url));
  context.startActivity(browserIntent);
}
```

14. Implement the methods to start an application using the following code:

```java
public void startApp(String packageName) {
  Intent intent = new Intent(packageName);

  try {
    context.startActivity(intent);
  } catch (ActivityNotFoundException e) {

    intent = new Intent(Intent.ACTION_VIEW);
    intent.setData(Uri.parse("market://details?id=" +
      packageName));
    context.startActivity(intent);
  }

}
```

15. Create a new class file named `SelectedActionsAdapter` with the following class members and constructor:

```java
private Context context;
private LayoutInflater layoutInflater;
private SparseArray<String> actions = new
  SparseArray<String>();

public SelectedActionsAdapter(Context context) {

  this.context = context;
  this.layoutInflater = (LayoutInflater)
    context.getSystemService
      (Context.LAYOUT_INFLATER_SERVICE);

}
```

16. Extend the `SelectedActionsAdapter` class from the `android.widget.BaseAdapter` class, and implement the following methods:

```java
@Override
public int getCount() {
  return actions.size();
}
```

```java
@Override
public Object getItem(int position) {
  return actions.get(actions.keyAt(position));
}


@Override
public long getItemId(int position) {
  return actions.keyAt(position);
}


@Override
public View getView(int position, View convertView,
  ViewGroup parent) {
  View listItem = convertView;

  if (convertView == null) {
    listItem = layoutInflater.inflate
      (android.R.layout.simple_list_item_1, null);
  }

  ((TextView) listItem.findViewById(android.R.id.text1)).
    setText(getItem(position).toString());

  return listItem;
}


public int[] getItemsId() {
  int[] keys = new int[actions.size()];

  for (int i = 0; i < actions.size(); i++) {
    keys[i] = actions.keyAt(i);
  }

  return keys;
}

  public void addItem(int actionIndex) {

    String[] actionsStrings =
      context.getResources().getStringArray(array.actions);

    actions.append(actionIndex,
      actionsStrings[actionIndex]);
```

```java
    notifyDataSetChanged();
  }


public void removeItem(int position) {
  actions.remove(actions.keyAt(position));
  notifyDataSetChanged();
}
```

17. Add the following class members to `MainActivity`:

```java
private NfcHelper nfcHelper;
private ActionHelper actionHelper;
private ProgressDialog waitingDialog;
private Spinner spinnerAction;
private ListView lstSelectedActions;
private SelectedActionsAdapter listAdapter;
```

18. Import the `NfcHelper.java` class into the project and enable the foreground dispatch system by overriding the `onResume` and the `onPause` methods using the following code:

```java
@Override
protected void onResume() {
  super.onResume();

  if (nfcHelper.isNfcEnabledDevice()) {
    nfcHelper.enableForegroundDispatch();
  }
}


@Override
protected void onPause() {
  super.onPause();

  if (nfcHelper.isNfcEnabledDevice()) {
    nfcHelper.disableForegroundDispatch();
  }
}
```

19. Implement the `OnItemSelectedListener` and `OnItemClickListener` interfaces in the `MainActivity` class:

```java
@Override
public void onItemSelected(AdapterView<?> parent, View
  view, int position, long id) {
```

```java
    if (position == 0) {
      return;
    }


    listAdapter.addItem(position);


  }


  @Override
  public void onNothingSelected(AdapterView<?> parent) {
    //no-op
  }


  @Override
  public void onItemClick(AdapterView<?> parent, View view,
    int position, long id) {


    listAdapter.removeItem(position);


  }
```

20. Initialize the class members using the following code:

```java
  @Override
  protected void onCreate(Bundle savedInstanceState) {
    ...


    nfcHelper = new NfcHelper(this);
    actionHelper = new ActionHelper(this);


    listAdapter = new SelectedActionsAdapter(this);


    spinnerAction = (Spinner)
      findViewById(R.id.spinnerAction);
    spinnerAction.setOnItemSelectedListener(this);


    lstSelectedActions = (ListView)
      findViewById(R.id.lstSelectedActions);
    lstSelectedActions.setAdapter(listAdapter);
    lstSelectedActions.setOnItemClickListener(this);
  }
```

21. Implement the `handleAction` method using the following code:

```java
private void handleAction(ActionHelper.Actions action) {

    switch (action) {
    case WIFI_ON:
      actionHelper.enableWifi();
      break;
    case WIFI_OFF:
      actionHelper.disableWifi();
      break;
    case BLUETOOTH_ON:
      actionHelper.enableBluetooth();
      break;
    case BLUETOOTH_OFF:
      actionHelper.disableBluetooth();
      break;
    case NAVIGATE_TO_PACKT_PUB:
      actionHelper.navigateToUrl("http://app.packtpub.com");
      break;
    case OPEN_PACKT_READER_APP:
      actionHelper.startApp
        ("za.co.snapplify.packtpublishing");
      break;
    case NONE:
    default:
      break;
    }

}
```

22. Implement the `handleIntent` method using the following code:

```java
private void handleIntent(Intent intent) {

    if (!nfcHelper.isNfcIntent(intent)) {
      return;
    }

    if (waitingDialog != null) {

      Integer count = listAdapter.getCount();

      NdefRecord[] records = new NdefRecord[count];
```

```java
          for (int i = 0; i < count; i++) {
            records[i] = NdefRecord.createExternal(
              "com.packtpub", "ch10example1type", new byte[] {
                (byte) listAdapter.getItemId(i) });
          }


          if (nfcHelper.writeNdefMessage(intent, new
            NdefMessage(records))) {
            Toast.makeText(this, R.string.toast_write_success,
              Toast.LENGTH_LONG).show();
          } else {
            Toast.makeText(this, R.string.toast_write_fail,
              Toast.LENGTH_LONG).show();
          }


          waitingDialog.dismiss();

        } else {

          NdefMessage ndefMessage =
            nfcHelper.getNdefMessageFromIntent(intent);

          for (NdefRecord ndefRecord :
            ndefMessage.getRecords()) {

            int actionId = ndefRecord.getPayload()[0];
            ActionHelper.Actions action =
              ActionHelper.Actions.values()[actionId];

            handleAction(action);

          }

          intent.removeExtra(NfcAdapter.EXTRA_NDEF_MESSAGES);
          intent.removeExtra(NfcAdapter.EXTRA_TAG);
        }

    }
```

23. Implement the write button-click event listener using the following code:

```java
public void onBtnWriteTagClick(View view) {

    if (listAdapter.getCount() == 0) {
        return;
    }

    displayWaitingDialog();
}
```

24. Implement the `displayWaitingDialog()` method using the following code:

```java
void displayWaitingDialog() {
    waitingDialog = new ProgressDialog(this);
    waitingDialog.setMessage(getString(
        R.string.dialog_waiting_tag));
    waitingDialog.setCancelable(true);
    waitingDialog.setOnDismissListener(new
        OnDismissListener() {

        @Override
        public void onDismiss(DialogInterface dialog) {

            waitingDialog = null;

        }
    });

    waitingDialog.show();
}
```

25. Call the `handleIntent` method in the `onResume` activity method using the following code:

```java
@Override
protected void onResume() {
    ...

    handleIntent(getIntent());

}
```

26. Override the `onNewIntent` method and add the following code:

```java
@Override
public void onNewIntent(Intent intent) {
  setIntent(intent);
}
```

27. Run the application and create a list of the desired actions.

28. Tap the tag on the phone or simulate a tap in NFC Simulator to write the tag.

29. Tap again on the written tag. The actions written should be performed.

How it works...

The `Actions` enumeration contains all the pre-programmed actions in the application that are made available to the user. To work with these actions, the user has to select them using a spinner. Then, we save the byte representation of the enumeration item ordinal number and create `NdefRecord` for each action. This way, we take advantage of one of the `NdefMessage` characteristics (there's a possibility you may have many `NdefRecord` instances with different contents and types).

When we tap a written tag on the smartphone, we get all the records present in the message; loop through them and convert them back to their `Action` representation. After that, the `handleAction` method gets called and the action is executed using the `ActionHelper` methods.

In this recipe, we used pre-programmed actions to demonstrate how we can create a multi-action tag, but a more generic behavior can be used; we can prompt the user to choose which URL or application to open.

There are many situations where a multi-action tag can be used. A simple example would be when we arrive home and we want to enable the Wi-Fi connection (which we probably disabled to save battery) and browse our favorite website. Or just before going to sleep, we will keep the device in the silent mode, set the wake up alarm, and so on. The tags can then be stuck in strategic places and used by everyone who has the application installed.

We can also use multiple `NdefRecord` instances to logically organize our data, as we did in the *Testing the tag data for integrity* recipe in *Chapter 8, Error Handling and Content Validation*.

Choosing the best format for our data

While developing other recipes, we have seen different ways of storing our data in an NFC tag. From a simple plain text to a raw object, it all depends on the data we need to store. In this recipe, we will learn about some other formats to store our data.

How to do it...

We will create several `NdefMessages` that contain a product representation in several formats by performing the following steps:

1. Open Eclipse and create a new Android application project named `NfcBookCh10Example2` and a package named `nfcbook.ch10.example2`.

2. Download the `google-gson` library from `https://code.google.com/p/google-gson/` and import the `.jar` file to the `libs` folder in the project.

3. Set the minimum SDK version to 16 using the following code:

```
<uses-sdk android:minSdkVersion="16" />
```

4. Add the strings given in the following code to the `strings.xml` file available at `res/values/`:

```
<string name="label_raw">Raw</string>
<string name="label_json">JSON</string>
<string name="label_raw_compressed">Raw Compressed</string>
<string name="label_raw_gzip">Raw GZIPed</string>
<string name="label_id">Product Id</string>
<string name="label_short_description">Short
  description</string>
<string name="label_json_compressed">JSON
  Compressed</string>
<string name="label_json_gziped">JSON GZIPed</string>
```

5. Replace the content of the `activity_main.xml` file located at `/res/layout` with the following code:

```
<RelativeLayout xmlns:android=
  "http://schemas.android.com/apk/res/android"
    xmlns:tools="http://schemas.android.com/tools"
    android:layout_width="match_parent"
    android:layout_height="match_parent"
    android:paddingBottom="@dimen/activity_vertical_margin"
    android:paddingLeft="@dimen/activity_horizontal_margin"
    android:paddingRight="@dimen/activity_horizontal_margin"
    android:paddingTop="@dimen/activity_vertical_margin"
    tools:context=".MainActivity" >

    <TextView
        android:id="@+id/textView9"
        android:layout_width="wrap_content"
        android:layout_height="wrap_content"
```

```xml
        android:layout_alignParentLeft="true"
        android:layout_alignParentTop="true"
        android:text="@string/label_id" />

    <EditText
        android:id="@+id/txtProductId"
        android:layout_width="wrap_content"
        android:layout_height="wrap_content"
        android:layout_alignParentLeft="true"
        android:layout_alignParentRight="true"
        android:layout_below="@+id/textView9"
        android:ems="10"
        android:inputType="number" >

        <requestFocus />
    </EditText>

    <TextView
        android:id="@+id/textView10"
        android:layout_width="wrap_content"
        android:layout_height="wrap_content"
        android:layout_alignParentLeft="true"
        android:layout_below="@+id/txtProductId"
        android:layout_marginTop="20dip"
        android:text="@string/label_short_description" />

    <EditText
        android:id="@+id/txtShortDescription"
        android:layout_width="wrap_content"
        android:layout_height="wrap_content"
        android:layout_alignParentLeft="true"
        android:layout_alignParentRight="true"
        android:layout_below="@+id/textView10"
        android:ems="10"
        android:inputType="text" />

    <TableLayout
        android:layout_width="wrap_content"
        android:layout_height="wrap_content"
        android:layout_alignParentBottom="true"
        android:layout_alignParentLeft="true"
        android:layout_alignParentRight="true"
        android:stretchColumns="1" >
```

```xml
<TableRow
    android:layout_width="wrap_content"
    android:layout_height="wrap_content" >

    <TextView
        android:layout_width="wrap_content"
        android:layout_height="wrap_content"
        android:layout_gravity="center"
        android:text="@string/label_type"
        android:textAppearance=
            "?android:attr/textAppearanceMedium" />

    <TextView
        android:layout_width="wrap_content"
        android:layout_height="wrap_content"
        android:layout_gravity="center"
        android:text="@string/label_message_size"
        android:textAppearance=
            "?android:attr/textAppearanceMedium" />
</TableRow>

<TableRow
    android:layout_width="wrap_content"
    android:layout_height="wrap_content" >

    <TextView
        android:layout_width="wrap_content"
        android:layout_height="wrap_content"
        android:text="@string/label_type_text" />

    <TextView
        android:id="@+id/lblTypeText"
        android:layout_width="wrap_content"
        android:layout_height="wrap_content"
        android:layout_gravity="right"
        android:textAppearance=
            "?android:attr/textAppearanceSmall" />
</TableRow>

<TableRow
    android:layout_width="wrap_content"
    android:layout_height="wrap_content" >

    <TextView
```

```xml
                android:layout_width="wrap_content"
                android:layout_height="wrap_content"
                android:text="@string/label_type_url" />

        <TextView
            android:id="@+id/lblTypeUrl"
            android:layout_width="wrap_content"
            android:layout_height="wrap_content"
            android:layout_gravity="right"
            android:textAppearance=
                "?android:attr/textAppearanceSmall" />
    </TableRow>

    <TableRow
        android:layout_width="wrap_content"
        android:layout_height="wrap_content" >

        <TextView
            android:layout_width="wrap_content"
            android:layout_height="wrap_content"
            android:text=
                "@string/label_type_external_type" />

        <TextView
            android:id="@+id/lblTypeExternal"
            android:layout_width="wrap_content"
            android:layout_height="wrap_content"
            android:layout_gravity="right"
            android:textAppearance=
                "?android:attr/textAppearanceSmall" />
    </TableRow>

    <TableRow
        android:layout_width="wrap_content"
        android:layout_height="wrap_content" >

        <TextView
            android:layout_width="wrap_content"
            android:layout_height="wrap_content"
            android:text="@string/label_external_json"
            />
```

```xml
        <TextView
            android:id="@+id/lblTypeExternalJson"
            android:layout_width="wrap_content"
            android:layout_height="wrap_content"
            android:layout_gravity="right"
            android:textAppearance=
              "?android:attr/textAppearanceSmall" />
    </TableRow>

    <TableRow
        android:layout_width="wrap_content"
        android:layout_height="wrap_content" >

        <TextView
            android:layout_width="wrap_content"
            android:layout_height="wrap_content"
            android:text=
              "@string/label_external_compressed" />

        <TextView
            android:id="@+id/lblTypeExternalCompressed"
            android:layout_width="wrap_content"
            android:layout_height="wrap_content"
            android:layout_gravity="right"
            android:textAppearance=
              "?android:attr/textAppearanceSmall" />
    </TableRow>

    <TableRow
        android:layout_width="wrap_content"
        android:layout_height="wrap_content" >

        <TextView
            android:layout_width="wrap_content"
            android:layout_height="wrap_content"
            android:text=
              "@string/label_external_json_compressed"
                />

        <TextView
            android:id=
              "@+id/lblTypeExternalJsonCompressed"
            android:layout_width="wrap_content"
```

```xml
            android:layout_height="wrap_content"
            android:layout_gravity="right"
            android:textAppearance=
              "?android:attr/textAppearanceSmall" />
    </TableRow>

    <TableRow>

        <TextView
            android:layout_width="wrap_content"
            android:layout_height="wrap_content"
            android:text="@string/label_external_gzip"
              />

        <TextView
            android:id="@+id/lblTypeExternalGzip"
            android:layout_width="wrap_content"
            android:layout_height="wrap_content"
            android:layout_gravity="right"
            android:textAppearance=
              "?android:attr/textAppearanceSmall" />
    </TableRow>

    <TableRow>

        <TextView
            android:layout_width="wrap_content"
            android:layout_height="wrap_content"
            android:text=
              "@string/label_external_json_gziped" />

        <TextView
            android:id="@+id/lblTypeExternalJsonGzip"
            android:layout_width="wrap_content"
            android:layout_height="wrap_content"
            android:layout_gravity="right"
            android:textAppearance=
              "?android:attr/textAppearanceSmall" />
    </TableRow>
  </TableLayout>

</RelativeLayout>
```

The preceding code creates a layout that is identical to that in the following screenshot:

6. Create a new class file named `Product`.

7. Add the following class fields to the `Product` class and the corresponding getters and setters:

```
private int Id;
private String ShortDescription;

public int getId() {
  return Id;
}

public void setId(int id) {
  Id = id;
}

public String getShortDescription() {
  return ShortDescription;
}
```

```java
public void setShortDescription(String shortDescription) {
  ShortDescription = shortDescription;
}


@Override
public String toString() {
  return String.format("{id}%s{description}%s", Id,
    ShortDescription);
}


public String toUrl() {
  return String.format(
    "com.packtpub:product?id=%s?description=%s", Id,
      ShortDescription);
}
```

8. Add the following class fields to `MainActivity` using the following code:

```java
private EditText txtProductId;
private EditText txtShortDescription;
private TextView lblTypeText;
private TextView lblTypeUrl;
private TextView lblTypeExternal;
private TextView lblTypeExternalJson;
private TextView lblTypeExternalCompressed;
private TextView lblTypeExternalJsonCompressed;
private TextView lblTypeExternalGzip;
private TextView lblTypeExternalJsonGzip;
```

9. Import the `NfcHelper.java` class into the project and enable the foreground dispatch system by overriding the `onResume` and the `onPause` methods using the following code:

```java
@Override
protected void onResume() {
  super.onResume();

  if (nfcHelper.isNfcEnabledDevice()) {
  nfcHelper.enableForegroundDispatch();
  }
}


@Override
protected void onPause() {
  super.onPause();
```

```java
  if (nfcHelper.isNfcEnabledDevice()) {
    nfcHelper.disableForegroundDispatch();
  }
}
```

10. Implement the `objectToBytes` method with the following code:

```java
private byte[] objectToBytes(Object obj) {
  ByteArrayOutputStream bos = new ByteArrayOutputStream();
  ObjectOutput out = null;

  try {
    out = new ObjectOutputStream(bos);
    out.writeObject(obj);

    out.close();
    bos.close();

  } catch (Exception e) {
    Log.e("objectToBytes", e.getMessage());
  }

  return bos.toByteArray();
}
```

11. Implement the `bytesToObject` method using the following code:

```java
private Object bytesToObject(byte[] bytes) {
  Object o = null;
  ByteArrayInputStream bis = new
    ByteArrayInputStream(bytes);
  ObjectInput in = null;

  try {
    in = new ObjectInputStream(bis);

    o = in.readObject();

    bis.close();
  } catch (Exception e) {
    Log.e("bytesToObject", e.getMessage());
  }
  return o;
}
```

Implement the compress method:

```java
public byte[] compress(int type, byte[] data) {

  byte[] output = new byte[] {};

  try {
    ByteArrayOutputStream outputStream = new
      ByteArrayOutputStream(data.length);

    if (type == 0) {

      Deflater deflater = new Deflater();
      deflater.setLevel(Deflater.BEST_COMPRESSION);
      deflater.setInput(data);
      deflater.finish();

      byte[] buffer = new byte[1024];
      while (!deflater.finished()) {
        int count = deflater.deflate(buffer);
        outputStream.write(buffer, 0, count);
      }

      deflater.end();

    } else if (type == 1) {

      GZIPOutputStream gzipOutputStream = new
        GZIPOutputStream(outputStream);
      gzipOutputStream.write(data);
      gzipOutputStream.close();

    } else {

    }

    output = outputStream.toByteArray();
    outputStream.close();

  } catch (Exception e) {
    Log.e("compress", e.getMessage());
  }

  return output;
}
```

12. Implement the `TextWatcher` interface using the following code:

```java
@Override
public void afterTextChanged(Editable s) {

    Product product = new Product();

    String productId = "" + txtProductId.getText();

    if (!productId.isEmpty()) {
      product.setId(Integer.parseInt(productId));
    }

    product.setShortDescription("" +
      txtShortDescription.getText());

    byte[] rawObject = objectToBytes(product);
    byte[] jsonObject = new
      Gson().toJson(product).getBytes(Charset.forName("UTF-
        8"));



    NdefMessage textNdefMessage =
      nfcHelper.createTextNdefMessage(product.toString());

    NdefMessage urlNdefMessage =
      nfcHelper.createUrlNdefMessage(product.toUrl());

    NdefMessage externalNdefMessage =
      nfcHelper.createExternalTypeNdefMessage(
        "ch10example1type", rawObject);

    NdefMessage externalJsonNdefMessage =
      nfcHelper.createExternalTypeNdefMessage(
        "ch10example1type", jsonObject);

    NdefMessage externalCompressedNdefMessage =
      nfcHelper.createExternalTypeNdefMessage(
        "ch10example1type", compress(0, rawObject));

    NdefMessage externalJsonCompressedNdefMessage =
      nfcHelper.createExternalTypeNdefMessage(
        "ch10example1type", compress(0, jsonObject));
```

```java
    NdefMessage externalGzipNdefMessage =
      nfcHelper.createExternalTypeNdefMessage(
        "ch10example1type", compress(1, rawObject));

    NdefMessage externalJsonGzipNdefMessage =
      nfcHelper.createExternalTypeNdefMessage(
        "ch10example1type", compress(1, jsonObject));


    lblTypeText.setText("" +
      textNdefMessage.getByteArrayLength());

    lblTypeUrl.setText("" +
      urlNdefMessage.getByteArrayLength());

    lblTypeExternal.setText("" +
      externalNdefMessage.getByteArrayLength());

    lblTypeExternalJson.setText("" +
      externalJsonNdefMessage.getByteArrayLength());

    lblTypeExternalCompressed.setText("" +
      externalCompressedNdefMessage.getByteArrayLength());

    lblTypeExternalJsonCompressed.setText("" +
      externalJsonCompressedNdefMessage.getByteArrayLength
        ());

    lblTypeExternalGzip.setText("" +
      externalGzipNdefMessage.getByteArrayLength());

    lblTypeExternalJsonGzip.setText("" +
      externalJsonGzipNdefMessage.getByteArrayLength());

  }

  @Override
  public void beforeTextChanged(CharSequence s, int start,
    int count, int after) {
    // no-op
  }

  @Override
  public void onTextChanged(CharSequence s, int start, int
    before, int count) {
```

```
    // no-op
  }
```

13. Initialize `nfcHelper` and the layout elements using the following code:

```
@Override
protected void onCreate(Bundle savedInstanceState) {

  ...
  nfcHelper = new NfcHelper(this);

  txtProductId = (EditText)
    findViewById(R.id.txtProductId);
  txtShortDescription = (EditText)
    findViewById(R.id.txtShortDescription);

  lblTypeText = (TextView) findViewById(R.id.lblTypeText);
  lblTypeUrl = (TextView) findViewById(R.id.lblTypeUrl);
  lblTypeExternal = (TextView)
    findViewById(R.id.lblTypeExternal);
  lblTypeExternalJson = (TextView)
    findViewById(R.id.lblTypeExternalJson);
  lblTypeExternalCompressed = (TextView)
    findViewById(R.id.lblTypeExternalCompressed);
  lblTypeExternalJsonCompressed = (TextView)
    findViewById(R.id.lblTypeExternalJsonCompressed);
  lblTypeExternalGzip = (TextView)
    findViewById(R.id.lblTypeExternalGzip);
  lblTypeExternalJsonGzip = (TextView) findViewById(R.
id.lblTypeExternalJsonGzip);

  txtProductId.addTextChangedListener(this);
  txtShortDescription.addTextChangedListener(this);
}
```

14. Run the application and fill in the product information.

How it works...

Simple plain texts are sufficient when we talk about a note or a Wi-Fi setting. However, when the data to store becomes more complex, it's not by far the best way to store it. In this recipe, we created several other ways to represent our data, some with a bigger footprint—such as the raw object—and other in a more human-readable format such as JSON. The decision on which method to use depends on the size available in the tags, on our data model, and on cross-application support.

Locking tags

Until now, we probably used and reused the same tags to write different content types during the implementation of recipes. There is absolutely no problem with that while we are in the development stage since we need to constantly test what we are doing. In real-life usage, we may need/want to prevent tag rewrites to prevent malicious users from changing the tag content.

How to do it...

We will make some changes in the `NfcHelper` class and allow the user to choose whether or not to make the tag read-only:

1. Open Eclipse and create a new Android application project named `NfcBookCh10Example3` and the package named `nfcbook.ch10.example3`.

2. Make sure the `AndroidManifest.xml` file is configured correctly. Refer to the *Requesting NFC permissions* recipe in *Chapter 1, Getting Started with NFC*.

3. Set the minimum SDK version to 16 using the following code:

   ```xml
   <uses-sdk android:minSdkVersion="16" />
   ```

4. Add the strings given in the following code to the `strings.xml` file located at `res/values/`:

   ```xml
   <string name="write_tag">Write tag</string>
   <string name="dialog_waiting_tag">Waiting tag...</string>
   <string name="toast_write_success">Tag written</string>
   <string name="toast_write_fail">Failed to write
     tag</string>
   <string name="tag_content">Tag content</string>
   <string name="type">Tag type</string>
   <string name="lock">Lock tag</string>
   <string name="cannot_undone">This cannot be
     undone!</string>

   <string-array name="array_tag_types">
     <item>Url</item>
     <item>Text</item>
   </string-array>
   ```

5. Replace the content of the `activity_main.xml` file located at `/res/layout` with the following code:

   ```xml
   <LinearLayout xmlns:android=
     "http://schemas.android.com/apk/res/android"
   ```

```xml
    xmlns:tools="http://schemas.android.com/tools"
    xmlns:app="http://schemas.android.com/apk/res-auto"
    android:layout_width="match_parent"
    android:layout_height="match_parent"
    android:orientation="vertical"
    android:paddingBottom="@dimen/activity_vertical_margin"
    android:paddingLeft="@dimen/activity_horizontal_margin"
    android:paddingRight=
      "@dimen/activity_horizontal_margin"
    android:paddingTop="@dimen/activity_vertical_margin"
    tools:context=".MainActivity" >

    <TextView
        android:id="@+id/textView1"
        android:layout_width="wrap_content"
        android:layout_height="wrap_content"
        android:text="@string/type"
        android:textAppearance=
          "?android:attr/textAppearanceMedium" />

    <Spinner
        android:id="@+id/spinnerType"
        android:layout_width="fill_parent"
        android:layout_height="wrap_content"
        android:entries="@array/array_tag_types" />

    <Switch
        android:id="@+id/switchLockTag"
        android:layout_width="match_parent"
        android:layout_height="wrap_content"
        android:layout_marginTop="20dip"
        android:text="@string/lock" />

    <TextView
        android:id="@+id/textView3"
        android:layout_width="wrap_content"
        android:layout_height="wrap_content"
        android:text="@string/cannot_undone"
        android:textAppearance=
          "?android:attr/textAppearanceSmall" />

    <TextView
        android:id="@+id/textView2"
        android:layout_width="wrap_content"
```

```
        android:layout_height="wrap_content"
        android:layout_marginTop="20dip"
        android:text="@string/tag_content"
        android:textAppearance=
           "?android:attr/textAppearanceMedium" />
    <EditText
        android:id="@+id/txtContent"
        android:layout_width="match_parent"
        android:layout_height="0dip"
        android:layout_weight="1"
        android:ems="10"
        android:inputType="textMultiLine" >

        <requestFocus />
    </EditText>

    <Button
        android:id="@+id/btnWriteTag"
        android:layout_width="match_parent"
        android:layout_height="wrap_content"
        android:onClick="onBtnWriteTagClick"
        android:text="@string/write_tag" />

</LinearLayout>
```

This creates a layout that is identical to that in the following screenshot:

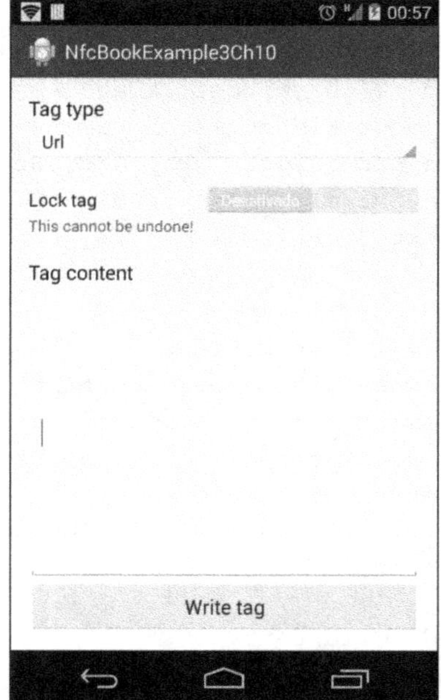

6. Add the following class members to `MainActivity`:

```
private NfcHelper nfcHelper;
private ProgressDialog waitingDialog;
private EditText txtContent;
private Spinner spinnerType;
private Switch switchLockTag;
```

7. Import the `NfcHelper.java` class into the project and enable the foreground dispatch system by overriding the `onResume` and the `onPause` methods:

```
@Override
protected void onResume() {
  super.onResume();

  if (nfcHelper.isNfcEnabledDevice()) {
    nfcHelper.enableForegroundDispatch();
  }
}

@Override
protected void onPause() {
  super.onPause();

  if (nfcHelper.isNfcEnabledDevice()) {
    nfcHelper.disableForegroundDispatch();
  }
}
```

8. Initialize `nfcHelper` and the layout elements using the following code:

```
@Override
protected void onCreate(Bundle savedInstanceState) {

  ...
  nfcHelper = new NfcHelper(this);

  txtContent = ((EditText) findViewById(R.id.txtContent));
  spinnerType = ((Spinner) findViewById(R.id.spinnerType));
  switchLockTag = ((Switch)
    findViewById(R.id.switchLockTag));
}
```

9. Implement the `makeTagReadonly` method in the `NfcHelper` class using the following code:

```java
public void makeTagReadonly(Intent intent) {

    Tag tag = getTagFromIntent(intent);

    try {

      if (tag != null) {

        Ndef ndef = Ndef.get(tag);

        if (ndef != null) {
          ndef.connect();

          if (ndef.canMakeReadOnly()) {
            ndef.makeReadOnly();
          }

          ndef.close();
        }
      }

    } catch (Exception e) {
      Log.e("makeTagReadonly", e.getMessage());
    }

}
```

10. Implement the `handleIntent` method using the following code:

```java
private void handleIntent(Intent intent) {

    if (!nfcHelper.isNfcIntent(intent)) {
      return;
    }

    if (waitingDialog != null) {

      NdefMessage ndefMessage;

      if (spinnerType.getSelectedItemPosition() == 0) {
```

```java
        ndefMessage = nfcHelper.createTextNdefMessage(
          txtContent.getText().toString());
      } else {
        ndefMessage = nfcHelper.createUrlNdefMessage(
          txtContent.getText().toString());
      }

      if (nfcHelper.writeNdefMessage(intent, ndefMessage))
        {

        if(switchLockTag.isChecked()){
          nfcHelper.makeTagReadonly(intent);
        }

        Toast.makeText(this, R.string.toast_write_success,
          Toast.LENGTH_LONG).show();
      } else {
        Toast.makeText(this, R.string.toast_write_fail,
          Toast.LENGTH_LONG).show();
      }

      waitingDialog.dismiss();

    }

  }
```

11. Implement the `displayWaitingDialog` method using the following code:

```java
void displayWaitingDialog() {
  waitingDialog = new ProgressDialog(this);
  waitingDialog.setMessage(getString(
    R.string.dialog_waiting_tag));
  waitingDialog.setCancelable(true);
  waitingDialog.setOnDismissListener(new
    OnDismissListener() {

    @Override
    public void onDismiss(DialogInterface dialog) {
      waitingDialog = null;
    }
  });

  waitingDialog.show();
}
```

12. Implement the write button-click event listener using the following code:

```
public void onBtnWriteTagClick(View view) {
   displayWaitingDialog();
}
```

13. Call the `handleIntent` method in the `onResume` activity method using the following code:

```
@Override
protected void onResume() {

   . . .

   handleIntent(getIntent());

}
```

14. Override the `onNewIntent` method and add the following code:

```
@Override
public void onNewIntent(Intent intent) {
   setIntent(intent);
}
```

15. Run the application; choose the desired content type and whether or not to lock the tag.

16. Tap on a tag on your phone or simulate a tap in the NFC Simulator to write the tag.

17. Try to rewrite the tag content. A **Failed to write tag** message should appear.

How it works...

We added a new method to `NfcHelper` that allows us to make an `Ndef` tag read-only. This method only gets called when the user sets the lock switch to **Enabled**. The actual tag locking happens when the `makeReadOnly` method from the `Ndef` class instance is called. After this method gets called, there is no turning back, unless the tag cannot be made read-only. We can check this using the `canMakeReadOnly` method—the tag is made read-only and its content cannot be changed.

This process sets a flag in the NFC tag's **capability container** (**CC**) that marks the contents as read-only and, where possible, permanently sets the lock bits to prevent any further modification of the memory. When the lock bits cannot be changed, an attacker would still be able to re-program the tag, although the CC files indicate that the tag is read-only.

Joking with a friend

A little healthy joke is always welcome and NFC can help you with that.

Getting ready

Make sure you have some imagination and your friend isn't going to be upset with a small joke.

How to do it...

We will simply write a troll-video URL into the tag by performing the following steps:

1. Open the application from the *Visiting our website* recipe in *Chapter 4, Writing Tag Content – Real-life Examples*, or any other application that allows us to write a URL to a tag.

2. Get a URL of a trolling video or image. I especially like the *10 Hour Video - Troll Song*.

3. Write the desired URL to the tag.

4. Find your victim and make an excuse or set a trap for them to tap on the tag.

How it works...

When we tap on a URL-formatted tag, Android will automatically open the browser without asking or prompting the user. This is the default behavior and allows us to rapidly navigate to a URL. In this recipe, we are taking advantage of the default behavior to troll our friends. Hope you have fun!

Thank you for buying
Near Field Communication with Android Cookbook

About Packt Publishing

Packt, pronounced 'packed', published its first book "*Mastering phpMyAdmin for Effective MySQL Management*" in April 2004 and subsequently continued to specialize in publishing highly focused books on specific technologies and solutions.

Our books and publications share the experiences of your fellow IT professionals in adapting and customizing today's systems, applications, and frameworks. Our solution based books give you the knowledge and power to customize the software and technologies you're using to get the job done. Packt books are more specific and less general than the IT books you have seen in the past. Our unique business model allows us to bring you more focused information, giving you more of what you need to know, and less of what you don't.

Packt is a modern, yet unique publishing company, which focuses on producing quality, cutting-edge books for communities of developers, administrators, and newbies alike. For more information, please visit our website: www.packtpub.com.

About Packt Open Source

In 2010, Packt launched two new brands, Packt Open Source and Packt Enterprise, in order to continue its focus on specialization. This book is part of the Packt Open Source brand, home to books published on software built around Open Source licences, and offering information to anybody from advanced developers to budding web designers. The Open Source brand also runs Packt's Open Source Royalty Scheme, by which Packt gives a royalty to each Open Source project about whose software a book is sold.

Writing for Packt

We welcome all inquiries from people who are interested in authoring. Book proposals should be sent to author@packtpub.com. If your book idea is still at an early stage and you would like to discuss it first before writing a formal book proposal, contact us; one of our commissioning editors will get in touch with you.

We're not just looking for published authors; if you have strong technical skills but no writing experience, our experienced editors can help you develop a writing career, or simply get some additional reward for your expertise.

Android Application Security Essentials

ISBN: 978-1-84951-560-3   Paperback: 218 pages

Write secure Android applications using the most up-to-date techniques and concepts

1. Understand Android security from kernel to the application layer.

2. Protect components using permissions.

3. Safeguard user and corporate data from prying eyes.

4. Understand the security implications of mobile payments, NFC, and more.

Android Development Tools for Eclipse

ISBN: 978-1-78216-110-3   Paperback: 144 pages

Set up, build, and publish Android projects quickly using Android Development Tools for Eclipse

1. Build Android applications using ADT for Eclipse.

2. Generate Android application skeleton code using wizards.

3. Advertise and monetize your applications.

Please check **www.PacktPub.com** for information on our titles

Raspberry Pi Home Automation with Arduino

ISBN: 978-1-84969-586-2   Paperback: 176 pages

Automate your home with a set of exciting projects for the Rasberry Pi!

1. Learn how to dynamically adjust your living environment with detailed step-by-step examples.

2. Discover how you can utilize the combined power of the Raspberry Pi and Arduino for your own projects.

3. Revolutionize the way you interact with your home on a daily basis.

Raspberry Pi Server Essentials

ISBN: 978-1-78328-469-6   Paperback: 116 pages

Transform your Raspberry Pi into a server for hosting websites, games, or even your Bitcoin network

1. Unlock the various possibilities of using Raspberry Pi as a server.

2. Configure a media center for your home or sharing with friends.

3. Connect to the Bitcoin network and manage your wallet.

Please check **www.PacktPub.com** for information on our titles